Sexual Chemistry

Sexual Chemistry

WHAT IT IS, HOW TO USE IT

BY JULIUS FAST AND MEREDITH BERNSTEIN

M. EVANS AND COMPANY, INC.   NEW YORK

Library of Congress Cataloging in Publication Data

Fast, Julius, 1918-
  Sexual chemistry.

  Bibliography: p.
  1. Sex (Psychology)   2. Sexual excitement.
3. Interpersonal attraction.   I. Bernstein, Meredith.
II. Title.
BF692.F34   1983   155.3   83-16389

ISBN 0-87131-417-7

M. Evans and Company, Inc.
216 East 49 Street
New York, New York 10017
Design by Lauren Dong
Manufactured in the United States of America
9 8 7 6 5 4 3 2 1

Contents

Foreword

Body Language was published in 1970, thirteen years ago, and since that time my life has changed in a number of ways. In addition to my writing, I became a guest on dozens of television shows, and I began to lecture to groups all over the United States—to businesspeople and students, lawyers and doctors, schoolteachers and auctioneers.

I have been asked to conduct industrial seminars, been involved in encounter groups and sensitivity sessions, have taught a number of classes on body language, and have been called in as a consultant by politicians and executives.

What to me seemed at first a very obvious thesis—we communicate with our bodies as well as our mouths—has mushroomed into an overwhelming occupation. I have had to probe deeper and deeper into the subject in order to keep up with my own field.

In addition to the lecturing and teaching, I have had many letters from people in every walk of life asking questions on every aspect of body language. Among the more intriguing letters I received were those from young Ph.D. candidates searching for various aspects of nonverbal communication to explore for their doctoral theses. A number of them questioned me about the body language of sexual attraction, how it worked and why it worked.

I was able to give them some direction in terms of research, but the very number of questions on this subject started me off on a new line of speculation. Just what is sexual attraction, or sexual chemistry? How does it work, and why? Is it completely a matter of psychology, or is there a biological basis to the attraction we humans feel for each other? Is sexual chemistry a physical matter involving receptors and receptor sites within the brain? What are the elements that make up sexual chemistry, and how do we use them?

Some years ago I did a medical motion picture for a drug company on the work of Dr. José Delgado at Yale University. Dr. Delgado, a neurophysiologist, had implanted electrodes in the pleasure center of rhesus monkeys, the same center that regulates sexual enjoyment, a part of the hypothalamus. He discovered that stimulation of these centers, by electricity or with chemicals, would cause sexual arousal, the animal equivalent of sexual chemistry in humans.

In the years that followed, I continued my research into sexual chemistry, questioning hundreds of men and women about their experience with love and attraction, compiling statistics, and gradually uncovering and understanding that mysterious force that can suddenly, and without warning, ignite immediate chemistry between two people.

In the course of my research I met Meredith Bernstein,

who for many years had been reading up on sexual chemistry. Meredith, who had gathered an impressive amount of data in the course of her research, seemed a natural collaborator. We combined our findings, and the writing of *Sexual Chemistry* was under way.

JULIUS FAST

Sexual Chemistry

1
What Is Sexual Chemistry?

AT FIRST SIGHT

"I think I should have known in advance that something was going to happen that night," Anne told us. "I was restless and uneasy. I had planned a pleasant night at home curled up with a good book, but I knew as soon as I left work that a comfortable night was impossible. I was too anxious and—yes, uneasy. I paced around the apartment, my lovely apartment that I had furnished so carefully, my refuge, as I had always thought of it—but that night my prison! I knew I had to get out, see people, go somewhere—anywhere!

"Then I remembered a discothèque I had visited with a friend a few weeks ago. The music there was mixed, half disco and half golden oldies, even some slow dance tunes from the forties and fifties, and the crowd was just as mixed: young people, old people, singles, partners—a place where you could feel comfortable alone or with a friend.

"After a few calls I found someone who was just as restless as I was, and Laura and I made our arrangements. It was just what I needed, the music, the crowd, the noise—all of it took me out of myself, and I settled down to an enjoyable evening."

Anne had found out long ago, she told us, that there was nothing devastating about going up to a perfect stranger and asking him if he'd like to dance. "Look, nine out of ten men are flattered if they're approached, and you simply can't worry about the tenth!"

Anne had been in the disco about an hour, dancing to some fast numbers and some slow ones, but she hesitated as the band struck up a waltz. That really wasn't her thing, and maybe she ought to sit it out. But even as she started for the table to join Laura, someone she hadn't noticed before asked, "Would you like to dance?"

"I turned, ready to refuse," she said with a little smile, "and then I met his eyes, and suddenly without warning I felt my heart begin to race and my legs grew weak. I'm not at all shy, but I had trouble speaking. I finally managed to say, 'Why don't we sit this one out—and talk?'"

"Whatever had hit me had hit him too. I could see it in his eyes, almost feel it in the tension that was suddenly between us. Without a word we walked over to one of the tables, sat down, and ordered two beers. Then we began to talk. Everything we said to each other, no matter how inane, was just right. We found ourselves telling each other things that were quite intimate."

His name, Anne found out, was Dan, and he was married and had two children. He showed her their pictures. He loved his wife and children, he told her. He was in town on business and had to leave the next day. It was all open and aboveboard, and they both knew that nothing serious could come of it, but they went back to Anne's apartment that night and slept together.

Shaking her head in a slightly bemused way, Anne said, "Sex between us was magical, wonderful. We both agreed it was just about perfect!"

"Have you seen him since?" we asked.

"Twice when he was in town, and there's still that uncanny attraction. We're not in love with each other, and neither of us wants a really serious relationship, but my God, there's a magic between us. I felt it that first time, and I feel it every time we meet."

THE PERFECT MATCH

What Anne described to us in that session isn't unique or even unusual. It has happened again and again, ever since Eve urged Adam to bite the apple. It's often called "love at first sight," for want of a better name. But we prefer to define it as "sexual chemistry." In Anne's case, as in numerous others, it happened without love. The two of them felt an overwhelming compulsion that drew them into bed.

There is no doubt that Anne was ready for it. She talked of feeling restless, uneasy, and imprisoned in her own home. She experienced a pent-up energy that was searching for a way to direct itself.

In discussing her reaction to the evening, we realized that we had just begun to open a Pandora's box on the subject of sexual chemistry. Neither Anne nor Dan had felt that their reaction, no matter how strong and sexual, was something that would break up Dan's marriage or interfere with Anne's life.

Research psychologists in the United States and Germany have established that there is a sound biological basis for the phenomenon of sexual chemistry. When we are sexually aroused, or when we meet someone who interests us intensely, when we experience that moment of understanding, our sympathetic nervous system begins to create the hormone norepinephrine in our nerve endings and in our adrenal glands.

Dr. Michael R. Liebowitz, assistant professor of clinical psychiatry at the College of Physicians and Surgeons at Columbia University, has done a great deal of research into the biological mechanisms that involve sexual chemistry. "Love depends on powerful perturbations of our normal brain chemicals," he has stated, and he points out that there are more than thirty neurotransmitters that bridge the synapses in our nerve cells.

Two of these, norepinephrine and dopamine, affect the pleasure center in the brain and are directly responsible for what we feel when we fall in love. Our breath comes faster, and there is a feeling of euphoria, a rapid pulse, a compulsion to talk, and a type of comfortable aggression that allows us to make advances we would ordinarily be too shy to consider. We feel excited, happy, and full of anticipation. Sexual chemistry has occurred!

The pleasure center, where all of this takes place, was discovered by Dr. José Delgado, a neurophysiologist at Yale University, in his research with rhesus monkeys. Many years ago he demonstrated to one of the authors his unusual findings. He had drilled through the skull of a monkey and inserted a tiny probe into the area of the brain's limbic system known as the pleasure center. He then rigged up a device that allowed the monkey to stimulate this pleasure center, the area responsible for emotional satisfaction. Watching Dr. Delgado's setup, the author saw the monkey repeatedly press the lever that sent a tiny electrical impulse into his brain. "He will give up food and drink and everything else to keep up that emotional stimulation," Dr. Delgado explained. "In the end, he can pleasure himself to death!"

Humans too, when some stimulus continually excites their pleasure center, will give up food and drink and grow "pale and wan" with love. The stimuli that excite the limbic region in humans are the two neurotransmitters norepinephrine and dopamine. In a manner we do not yet fully understand, they work on a naturally occurring amphetaminelike substance in the brain called phenylethylamine, and the triggering agent is that moment of sudden awakening, that emotional reaction, that starts it all.

There is, then, a chemical reaction within our bodies, produced by our own excitement, that begins at the level of our neuroreceptors. This reaction, in turn, by stimulating our nervous system even further, intensifies that unique and excited feeling of "sexual" chemistry. We are "tuned in and turned on" in the true, chemical sense of the phrase.

As we continued our research and talked to other people who had felt the same compelling attraction, we found that as often as sexual chemistry was devoid of love, it was equally often a part of love. For example, there were Douglas and Jane, another couple we interviewed.

"We met at college," Doug recalls. "It was in our senior year, but Jane was living with Michael off campus, and I was having a heavy affair with Gloria. Mike was my best friend and I wasn't about to poach on his territory, and Jane respected Gloria, so the two of us ate our hearts out and never dated each other.

"Three years after graduation I was working in Boston for an engineering firm when I got a call from Jane. She had broken up with Michael and driven east to look for work. She was in Boston, and could she crash at my place. Gloria, whom I sent Christmas cards to, had given her my address.

"I said, 'Of course,' and she came, and I opened the door, and the two of us just stared so hungrily we almost devoured each other with our eyes. That old magic was still there, untouched, unchanged! She came into my arms without a word. What can I tell you? We lived together only as long as it took to get the wedding invitations in the mail!"

"That old magic," we asked Doug. "What was it?"

He shrugged uneasily. "I don't know. I can't put my finger on it exactly. Well, this sounds crazy, but it's as if the two of us were made out of one piece that had somehow been broken apart, and our meeting was a perfect match, the coming together of two pieces to make a whole."

MAN TO MAN

Curiously, Doug's description of what he and Jane felt is much like the description a chemist once gave us of a chemical reaction. "There's a chemical bond between two atoms when the forces acting between them are strong enough. That bond can pull two different substances together to form something new and different."

That something "new and different" is the state Anne and Dan found themselves in the moment they met. Jane and Doug took three years to get together, but the bond was there between them, waiting only for the right moment to act. With Anne and Dan there was no love, only the chemical attraction. With Joan and Doug there was love as well, but it made the bond permanent. When sexual chemistry works with love, it is enhanced and given the touch of romance that literature is so fond of, but it can work without love. The strange thing about it is that it works not only between man and woman, but between two members of the same sex as well.

In his novel *The Chosen* Chaim Potok describes the sexual chemistry that draws two young men to each other with an irresistible force. There is nothing homosexual in the bond; it is an insistent, almost devouring friendship erupting out of anger and hurt. This type of male friendship, or bonding, is not new. It existed long before the story of David and Jonathan immortalized it in the Bible. It is a friendship that often occurs immediately and crosses every boundary of class, wealth, and origin.

"I met Tom at West Point," Peter told us. "The first day we arrived. I don't know what it was, but we took one look at each other and smiled—and that was it. Tom comes from Tennessee, from a poor mountain family, and I'm a New York boy, born and raised in Manhattan. You know, we've got nothing in common—what the hell can we talk about? And yet when we're together we don't shut up for a minute.

"I took Tom home over the Thanksgiving vacation, and my parents were charmed at first. He looked so great in his uniform. But Mom took me aside later and asked me, 'What on earth are you two doing together, Peter? You're like day and night.' And we are, but Christ, all I know is that when we're together I'm happy, and Tom feels the same way."

We asked him if there was anything physical in the relationship, and he shook his head. "You know, it's funny, I could understand it better if there was. Hey, when I was married Tom was my best man, and I'm going to be at his wedding next June. Right now we're pulling strings so we can be stationed near each other."

When we asked him to try to describe what he felt, he shrugged. "How do I feel about Tom? I don't know what to say. It's just a sense of comfort when we're together, completion, a kind of belonging. Right now our biggest problem is whether our wives will get along. I sure hope so, because otherwise . . ." His voice trailed off and he looked at us with a comic air. "I just don't know."

The same sense of completeness that Jane and Doug felt, but without the sexual connection, existed between Tom and Peter, and yet it was a kind of sexual chemistry that bound them together. Traditional literature is filled with stories of men who have found that same magical bond, and now, as women begin to find a new strength in feminism, we hear more and more of the same bond between women.

The literature that women are producing today often focuses on that bond. There is, in effect, a "new girl" network of female interdependence being established, from child rearing to business affairs.

THE MUTUAL FACTOR

For sexual chemistry to work, it must be mutual; it must occur in both people. If only one person feels that instant attraction, then there is no chemistry involved. It's as if, to get back to our chemical analogy, you put an active chemical in with an inert one. Nothing would happen, no matter what methods you used. But put two active chemicals together and use the correct techniques—heat, electricity, water, or whatever—and your chemical reaction takes place.

In the same way, put two people together who feel an instant attraction for each other, apply the right techniques, and sexual chemistry occurs. However, this doesn't mean that sexual chemistry must always occur in the first moment of meeting, or even the first weeks or months of meeting. It can lie dormant for a long time before, under the right conditions, it suddenly comes alive.

Take Pamela and Richard. "We first met at the lake," Pamela told us. "A friend had rented a large house for the summer, and each weekend a group of us from Chicago would chip in and share the house. Richard was one of the group, and while he looked good in a bathing suit, so did most of the men. All in all, it was like nothing. Here was this ordinary-looking guy, a lawyer, one of the girls said, coming on to me, and when I talked to him I didn't feel any . . . you know, any of the right vibes.

"Then, months later, I ran into him again—at his office, in fact. I was having a legal problem with my landlord, and a friend insisted I see this lawyer she knew. 'He's absolutely terrific,' she said. 'I used him when I divorced Jim, and it was the smartest thing I ever did.' Well, I went to see him, and of course it was Richard. I didn't recognize him at first in that three-piece suit with his tie and glasses. I'd only seen him at the lake in a bathing suit and sweat shirt, and this was a different man altogether. I watched him go over my lease and then get on the phone, and I was stunned, but delighted. In fifteen minutes he had straightened the whole thing out!

"There was a sense of power and certainty about him, and that turned me on, and I suddenly looked at him in a different way." She reached over and took his arm, pulling him close. "That did it!"

Richard laughed. "I felt *that* way the first time I met Pamela at the lake, but I realized there was nothing doing. I wasn't getting through. That day in my office was suddenly different. I could see the chemistry working, and I thought, this is going to be it—and it was! Don't ask me why. I asked her out to dinner that evening, ostensibly to talk over the case, but that was a line. I just knew I wanted to get to know her. I could feel that it was mutual, too."

Something had suddenly and unexpectedly turned Pamela on as far as Richard was concerned, and sexual chemistry came into being. It wasn't an attraction at first sight, or one that had to be hidden for a long time, but a sudden change in Pamela's perception that allowed this feeling between them to ignite. Seeing him in his own setting, wielding the power and knowledge of his job, she perceived a totally different, dynamic image. That changed something in her and allowed her to respond differently.

ACTING THE PART

The change in Pamela's perception of Richard brings up the question of whether sexual chemistry can be produced at will. Could Richard have projected a different image of himself at their very first meeting? Can anyone project that certain mixture of elements that ignites the spark, or is the ability to do so a part of our personality?

Among the people we interviewed were a number of actors, and one, a well-known stage and screen actor, felt that the ability to arouse sexual chemistry had to be an integral part of a person.

"You can't project that chemistry on the stage or screen unless you have it," he maintained. "It's not something you can fake or call up with Method acting. It has to be a part of you. There are actors who illuminate the screen with it. Cary Grant is one. I met him at a restaurant the other day, and even in his seventies he has that chemistry. Jean Harlow had it, and Marilyn Monroe had it, too, along with a quality of vulnerability. Both were telling the audience two things at the same time: I can have the world—and you can make me suffer!

"The actor who played opposite Monroe in *Bus Stop,* Don Murray, had it, and so did Jimmy Dean and Marlon Brando. Burt Reynolds has it today. But I maintain it can't be faked. Helen Hayes, splendid actress that she is, never had it, nor did George Lazenby, whom they tried to use to replace Sean Connery in the James Bond movies. Instead of igniting, he fizzled out!"

One of the actresses who projects that sense of sexual chemistry very successfully is Catherine Deneuve. That elusive magic occurs between her and most of the men who see her on the screen—and many of the women. Taking advantage of her ability to create sexual chemistry with an audience, Chanel Perfumes hired her, some time ago, to represent them in advertising. Her exquisite face stared out at us from advertisements in newspapers and magazines, and she spoke and smiled and looked languorous on the television screen.

"Chanel did very well with Deneuve," an advertising friend in the know told us, "but eventually they changed agencies—or account executives, I don't know which— and they replaced Deneuve with another type of ad—and their sales dropped. I hope to hell they get her back."

Surprised, we asked, "Do you have stock in Chanel?"

"Hell no, but I adore that woman! I can sit in front of the TV set, and when she comes on—believe me, I come on too!"

This ability to use sexual chemistry to sell a product is nothing new. How many cars are paired with beautiful young girls? And *young* isn't always the operative word. Witness the recent spate of ads with Lauren Bacall for Fortunoff. The curious thing about all these advertisements is that while in many cases the ads are aimed at the opposite sex, in just as many they are aimed at the same sex. Deneuve sold perfume to women; male models sell clothes to men. But of course it makes sense when we realize that sexual chemistry works between two men or two women as well as it works between a man and a woman.

The idea of using sexual chemistry to sell a product is not new. It may well have been started by the first Neanderthal who began to plug his own flints to his fellow cavemen. Certainly it was used to sell Caesar to the Romans, Arthur to the Britons, Napoleon to Europe, and in modern times Hitler seduced a nation with his own brand of sexual chemistry, just as Aimee Semple McPherson used hers and Billy Graham uses his in the name of religion. There was no question about John F. Kennedy's ability to ignite sexual chemistry, just as there's no doubt about Jimmy Carter's failure to do so.

Men or women who lecture, preach, or in other ways address people must be able to ignite that spark of sexual chemistry or risk losing their students, converts, or other audience. Recently, at a convention of auctioneers in Harrisburg, one of us spoke to the secretary of the group at dinner.

Blaine is outgoing and energetic and has the ability to project a kind of sexual chemistry to his audience at an auction. "You have to make them trust you, accept you, believe in you," he explained. "When any one of us is up before a potential group of buyers we flirt and carry on very much like an actor in the movies or on a stage.

"Now, some of us have no trouble doing it. We're 'on' whether we're up on the block or down among friends. But you would be amazed how many auctioneers are very shy, quiet guys who only come alive and project their charm when they're selling. It's a technique you learn—you have to learn."

The auctioneers Blaine talked about didn't fake their sexual chemistry. They learned to acquire it. A psychologist who specializes in treating sexual disorders acknowledged to us that the covering up of sexual chemistry in her patients often contributed to, or was responsible for, sexual dysfunction. "Part of my job is to teach them how to uncover it, how to light that very particular fire."

Remembering what our actor friend had said, we asked, "But isn't the ability to create that feeling a part of our personality, something you have or haven't?"

"Yes indeed." She nodded. "But you have to remember that personality is not fixed. It can change and be changed. You can certainly learn how to use sexual chemistry—once you know what it is."

A UNIVERSAL PHENOMENON

At this point we, as researchers, drew back. The material that was being revealed confirmed our fears that it would not be easy to define sexual chemistry. As we talked to more and more people, we began to understand that it achieves its effect empirically. However, we hoped to distill out its components and understand how and why it motivated everyone.

We discovered, in all of our interviews, that sexual chemistry needs the right elements to take place, the right energy, enthusiasm, and strength. In fact, these three elements are part and parcel of sexual chemistry. They must exist either in ourselves or in the people we are attracted to—and optimally in both.

Usually, although not always, there is a dominant-submissive element in sexual chemistry. The passive person rarely attracts others, rarely projects that exciting quality. But the submissive partner in a relationship can be energetic, enthusiastic, and, paradoxically, strong. Very often there is a strength in submission.

We tend, erroneously, to think of submission as a female trait—the dominant man, the submissive woman. The reverse, a submissive man and a dominant woman, has just as often resulted in profound and lasting sexual chemistry. The confusion of dominant-feminine-masculine-submissive must be straightened out. In the course of this book, we intend to rethink submission and see it as it really is, limited to neither sex and often possessing an active attribute.

Sexual chemistry, we have concluded after numerous interviews and extended research, is an interaction between two active partners who perceive in each other a mutual desire to fulfill an undefined, and perhaps primitive, need.

It is, in essence, a combination of many things: the way you look, the image you project, the way you talk, and even the way you think, the gestures you use—the total impact of your *self*. It is also the energy and enthusiasm you feel, and your strength—and sometimes weakness.

It can occur between lovers, or between people who aren't and will never be in love. It can occur between the sexes or within the same sex. It can be used to move masses, influence audiences, or get you what you want in a business situation. It is political and personal, and while it may work on one person, it may leave another cold!

2
Beyond the Spoken Word

THE EYES HAVE IT

Our eyes may or may not be the windows of our souls, but they are certainly our most eloquent instruments of communication, and in sexual chemistry they are the most important. That first spark is struck through the eyes. There is an instant of recognition, a moment that tells you that what you see is good, that here is someone very special, someone you would like to know, or someone who arouses you sexually—perhaps someone you could understand and who, in turn, could understand you.

All that in a single second of eye contact, but beyond that recognition factor there is the communication that takes place with eye contact. At a large cocktail party recently, we ran into an old friend, a very attractive young woman. After the usual "How have you been?" and "What's new?" we asked, "Are you free after the party? Perhaps we could have dinner."

She nodded across the room. "Do you see that tall blond guy there, the one talking to our hostess? Well, I'm leaving with him."

"A nice-looking fellow. Have you known him long?"

"Long?" She laughed. "I never met him. I haven't even talked to him yet. It's just one of those things. You know, 'across a crowded room' . . ."

"You're picking him up without a word?"

"It's mutual. You watch."

And we did. While neither approached the other, there were plenty of significant looks, and about a half hour later our friend caught the blond stranger's eye, looked at the clock, then glanced at the apartment door. Then she gave us a smile, collected her coat, said good-bye to the hostess, and went out the door. With impeccable timing, the blond stranger had managed to be there and leave with her at just that moment, and all, to our delight, without a word being spoken.

It was clearly a case of the simplest and the most eloquent body language. The eye contact to feel each other out came first. For every situation there is a *moral looking time.* That is the length of time you can hold someone's eye and still be within the bounds of propriety. Violate that time by even a second and you send a message. The message is usually *I am interested in you.*

How long is the moral looking time? It varies from no time at all in an elevator to an extremely long time when you are addressing an audience. The important fact is that each of us knows the moral looking time for every situation, if not instinctively, then by learning, even as we know the spoken language. Looking times are part of the vast, unspoken body language we use constantly, and they vary from culture to culture. In some African cultures they are extravagantly long, in the northern cultures rather short.

By catching the blond stranger's eye and holding eye contact for longer than the permitted time, my friend was saying *I like you* and setting in motion her own brand of sexual chemistry. She used her eyes first to size him up and then to transmit a message. In turn, as an indication that the sexual chemistry was working, her pickup allowed that lengthened eye contact.

If he had broken it off he would, in effect, have been saying *I am not interested,* and that would have been that. But he was interested, and sexual chemistry was ignited, and he not only held her gaze but returned it at other opportunities, and he added another signal—a smile.

Oh, that smile, that ubiquitous, exquisitely useful smile! It said not only *I am interested* but *I like what I see. I want to pursue this flirtation a bit further,* and she, knowing the silent language, returned the smile.

The final message, after almost an hour of flirtatious eye contact, was the glance at the clock and then at the door. It said, as plain as words, . . . *And away we go.*

"Why didn't you simply go up to him after the initial eye contact?" I asked her a few days later, when she was telling me what a wonderful evening she had had and all the plans the two of them were making. "Or for that matter, why didn't he come up to you? My God, it was a cocktail party, where you're supposed to talk to other guests."

She grinned rather wickedly. "Because this was more fun. This was sharing a secret the two of us had. We both knew something was simmering from that first moment, but we wanted to prolong it, to stretch it out as long as possible. It's a little like foreplay. The longer it goes on the more exciting the climax. We didn't say a word going down in the elevator, and I waited while he hailed a cab, and it was only then . . . well, that started it.''

"Oh no," I corrected her. "Your first look started it!''

And that first look always does—if it's to be started at all. If one person ignores the initial eye contact, nothing will happen, but if that person accepts the challenge— and it is a challenge—for any reason at all, there is a chance that sexual chemistry will take place.

Now the same two people who in one situation may react very strongly may in another, with nothing changed except that initial moment of contact, never react at all. If this is so, we have to reconsider sexual chemistry and realize that it is, to get back to our original chemical analysis, a reaction that needs the proper stimulus.

With inorganic chemicals, that stimulus could be heat, electricity, water; with sexual chemistry, a stimulus is also necessary. It can be eye contact, or any one of a number of elements we will consider more carefully in later chapters: general body language, clothes, the image we project, metacommunication, power, vulnerability, and many others. Any one of these elements, or a combination of them, can initiate the reaction. With my friend at the cocktail party it was eye contact. With Stephanie it was a smile.

THE UBIQUITOUS SMILE

Stephanie, a clinical psychologist with two nubile daughters, told us she had a lot of trouble getting through to her children. "Of course, everyone has," she said. "It's the name of the parenthood game. As a psychologist

I should know that. But now my girls are beginning to go
to school dances, not yet dating, you know—they're
fourteen and fifteen, and they go out in groups. Anyway,
they would come home from the dances devastated,
swearing they'll never go to another. 'None of the boys
talk to us or look at us!' That's their most common
complaint, and of course it's nonsense, as I realized when
I went to one dance to pick them up. They're very
attractive, and all the boys look at them—but that's as far
as it goes.

"That night I sat them down and said, 'Before I met
Daddy I was like you two girls. I'd go to parties or dances
and never have a boy say more than one or two words.'

"They looked at me appraisingly, for the first time
prepared to listen seriously to the old lady from another
generation. 'Do you know why?' I asked them, and they
shook their heads. 'Because I was dumb enough to think
that if I showed the boys how clever I was, how bitterly
ironical and cynical I could be, they'd be overwhelmed
by my intellect. So when one tried to talk to me, I'd look
at him coldly and come up with a brilliant one-liner that
was snotty and superior.'

"I saw their faces get that grudgingly intent look.
'What happened?'

"I shrugged. 'They'd back off and leave me alone, and
I'd go home and cry. Then one night—I don't know
why—a boy came up to me, and instead of cutting him
down I smiled at him. What a revelation! It was instant
attraction. For the first time I danced every number and
had the sense to keep my brilliant wit under wraps.' "

"Did your girls accept your advice?"

Stephanie laughed. "Not then, of course. It was 'Oh,
Mom!' and the eyes rolled up to the ceiling, but I notice

they've stopped complaining about dances, and they're getting a lot of phone calls from boys, and they keep telling me about these sudden, wild crushes of theirs—your sexual chemistry, I guess.''

FEEDBACK

The smile most certainly did it for Stephanie's girls. Eye contact can offer a hope, send a message, but the message is *I am interested in you,* no more. If one man violates the moral looking time with another man on the street, he is sending that same message—and it might be an insult, or an invitation to a homosexual pickup. But it can also be *Don't I know you?* or *There's something unusual/funny/startling about you.*

The eye contact followed by a smile changes the tone of the message. On the street it becomes *Hello.* In a small town, prolonged eye contact followed by a smile is a very common message. On a big-city street where paranoiac suspicions run high it's a tricky signal to use, even when a man uses it to a woman. The annoyed answer is usually *Is he trying to pick me up?*

But in a social situation it becomes a pleasant message to man or woman. *Let's talk. I like you. I want to know you. You're the only one here worth talking to,* and, when all other elements are right, *I am sexually attracted to you!*

The smile following eye contact was something a young friend of ours, Peter, learned in one of the authors' classes on body language. ''I'm a great one for singles bars,'' Peter confessed to us. ''But somehow I never seem to make out, or hit it off just right. I never felt that sexual chemistry you've been talking about—or when I felt it the girl never did. I'd talk to a girl and she'd seem interested at first, but after a few minutes, nothing. I'd see her eyes wander away and it was like a curtain came down between us."

We were a little surprised, because Peter was an attractive young man, dark with those bedroom eyes so many girls find romantic. "Now that you've taken the course," we asked him, "what's happened? Are things any better, singles-bar-wise?"

Peter grinned. "You bet they are. That course changed my life."

"In what way?"

"Well, first there was the eye-contact bit. Before, I used to go into a bar and spend half the night trying to find a girl who was receptive. Now I know that any girl who lets me make eye contact beyond the moral looking time isn't going to freeze up. She's willing to talk to me. I use the smile to let her know how I feel."

"Is that something new?"

"Hey man, before this I'd never smile. I didn't think it was cool, but I smile now, and then I go over and talk to her—well, that's where the big difference comes in."

"What's that?"

Peter frowned. "I could never understand why girls turned off when I talked to them until I learned about feedback. For some reason or other I didn't nod when I talked to people. Just learning to nod has made all the difference in the world."

That subtle nod that almost all of us use in conversation signals the other person, *Yes, I'm listening. I agree. You're right,* and so on. When you receive it, although you may not be aware of it, you feel the other person is sympathetic. If you don't receive it you feel as if you're talking to a stone wall. In sexual chemistry, the most intense attraction can be dampened before it ever takes off when there is no feedback, no nodding.

THE UPTIGHT STANCE

There is, then, in sexual chemistry, an entire silent body language that must be used before that quick attraction takes place. We've discussed the importance of eye contact, of the smile, and of feedback, but there are other elements of body language. There is the open position versus the closed, uptight position. Peter's inability to nod allowed for no feedback from any of the women he met, and thus resembled the closed, rigid posture of one of the women we interviewed.

"I don't understand why I have so much trouble making friends," Karen told us. "I'm lonely, and Lord knows I need friendship and companionship, but there are times when I feel I'm completely alone in a cold, alien world, and as far as sexual attraction goes, forget it. Oh, I've felt it often enough, but no one ever seems to feel it for me!"

Even as she talked to us, Karen seemed distant, cold, and slightly hostile. We had videotaped the session, and later we played it back to her. "Now watch yourself," we told her. "Is there anything about the way you sit, the way you gesture, that strikes you as unfriendly?"

After a few moments Karen said, "Please! Turn off the videotape. Something is terribly wrong. I'm not like that at all, I know I'm not!"

"Like that" was the sum of Karen's entire posture. She sat rigidly, her shoulders hunched slightly forward,

her arms clasped in front of her as she talked. She was
smoking during the interview, but she barely unclasped
her arms to put the cigarette in her mouth. Her entire
posture gave the impression of someone tight, rigid, and,
above all, inaccessible.

"Physically," we told her, "it's almost as if you were
curled up into a ball. Your knees are close together, your
arms pulled into your body. Even your face has a forbid-
ding look, and you didn't smile once during our entire
talk."

Karen bit her lip, and her eyes filled. "But I'm not like
that! I'm *not* cold and unfriendly. When I saw myself on
the monitor I was horrified. That's not me!"

Perhaps not, but it was Karen's body and Karen's
body language we were watching, and it sent out a clear-
cut message: *I don't want anything to do with you.*

One of the questions we confronted in our study was
why so many people sent contradictory messages with
their body, messages that were the exact opposite of what
they felt. After all, body language is unconscious and
should, therefore, be more honest, more direct than the
spoken language.

But it would be simplistic to assume that because
someone like Karen insisted that she wanted to make
contact with people that was the truth. An unconscious
part of Karen dreaded that contact and sabotaged every
effort to reach out and show warmth and understanding.

We were able to change Karen's attitude with a careful
explanation of what she was doing to give the wrong
impression, and with her cooperation. But although we
changed her body language and made it easier for her to
relate to people, the significant change had to come from
within herself. There had to be a change in the way she

perceived other people, particularly men. There had to be a change in her unconscious self. She had to really want the warmth and love on an unconscious as well as on a conscious level.

Once we had explained some of the basic errors Karen was making—the folded arms, her rigid posture, the closed-in, cold expression of her face—she began to change. It took a conscious effort on her part to learn to smile more readily, to sit in an open posture rather than a defensive one, to incline her body toward someone when she was talking to him, but very gradually she learned these little tricks, and as she learned them a curious thing happened: the new, more open image that Karen was faking began to change her rather tight and rigid personality. She began to feel looser, friendlier, able to make eye contact with greater confidence—and this, in turn, opened her body language.

We knew that she had come a long way when she reported her first encounter with sexual chemistry. "It was on a bus," she told us. "I was sitting across from this man, and there was something about him that I just liked. I guess part of it was the way he was dressed, with a sheepskin jacket and tight but very clean jeans and one of those cowboy hats—you knew he was a city guy, but enjoying the make-believe-cowboy rig. We kept making fleeting eye contact, sort of appraising each other, and then I told myself, what the hell—and I caught his eye and held it and, would you believe it, smiled!

"I did none of those awful uptight things that always closed me up, and he smiled back, and I felt a funny warmth spread right up from my legs." She laughed. "In that moment I knew what you were talking about. A funny, euphoric mood seemed to hit me. If I were a bit more courageous, if I had come a bit farther, I would have said something, but I just couldn't. But he felt it too, and I knew that whatever was blocking me was gone.''

Nothing came of Karen's first encounter with sexual chemistry, but it did show her that she could overcome the wall of resistance she had always built around her. It showed her that not only could she experience sexual chemistry, she could ignite it in someone else.

We talked about this circular effect of body language, its ability to change the way you felt, with a psychiatrist who has been involved in helping people overcome shyness. He pointed out that what had happened to Karen was a basic part of the therapy he used. ''If people are desperately shy, my job is to convince them that venturing a step toward extroversion won't destroy them. In fact, if it succeeds, it will strengthen them for the next step.

''Part of the therapy I use is changing their body language. I teach them to stand up straight, for example, and you'd be amazed how just that one little change in posture feeds back to their inner self, and they feel a bit stronger, a bit more outgoing. In the same way, if I change their body language to a more open type, a more receptive type, as you did with your friend Karen, they will become a little more receptive themselves.''

THE TENDER TOUCH

There was a study done recently in a public library by a group of researchers trying to discover the importance of touch. They had a librarian stamp outgoing books in two different manners. At first she did it in the normal way, with no contact between her and the borrower, simply stamping the books and handing them back. Then she changed her technique: each time she stamped a book and handed it to the borrower she allowed some contact to be made, even as simple a contact as brushing the borrower's hand as the book was taken.

Researchers stationed outside the library stopped the borrowers as they left and asked them for an appraisal of the library services. They asked a number of questions, among them an appraisal of the librarian. They pretended the questionnaire was a checkup on how the library functioned.

They discovered that whenever the librarian allowed that little touch, no matter how brief, she was thought of as warmer and more understanding than when she didn't. Evidently touch, no matter how fleeting, makes a great impression on the person touched. In sexual chemistry, touch has an invaluable place. It is one of the elements that can change your entire perception of someone else—or that person's perception of you.

Many politicians are aware of this, and "pressing the flesh" has come to be accepted as a valid method of convincing the voters of a politician's sincerity. The fashion is not only to shake the hand, but to make additional contact by grasping the forearm with your other hand.

We once knew a woman who was extremely skillful at this. Very ordinary in looks and personality, she still had a reputation among men as a very special person. At parties men would search her out, usually to settle down in some corner for an intimate talk.

Watching her and analyzing her methods, it became

clear that in addition to eye contact and an open posture, she used touch very skillfully. She would allow her thigh to brush against that of the man she was talking to, her hand to touch his arm—never the type of touch that would be noticed, but gentle, almost subliminal touching. It had its effect, however, in creating a matrix where sexual chemistry could occur, and indeed it did!

There is, of course, a right way and a wrong way to touch. Some people intuitively have "the touch." They know the psychologically correct moment to put an arm around your shoulders, to take your hand, to touch your back.

California salesman Barrie Stein had a record-breaking reputation in sales. Examining his approach, he realized that he would always touch the arm of a prospective buyer during his sales pitch. To check out the efficacy of this technique, he divided his sales staff into two groups. He had one group always touch the arm of a prospective client. The other group made no touching contact at all.

Eight months and a thousand sales pitches later, he discovered that the touchers averaged a sale eight out of every ten tries, while the nontouchers sold only three out of every ten!

This approach has been tried with many other groups, including recruiters for the United States Marine Corps. Major John Studenka of San Diego increased the recruiting ability of his officers by 114 percent by applying a touching technique to potential recruits. As to a possible way it works, salesman Stein suggests that touching is a comfort to the sensory nerves in the skin. "People want to be touched, and it triggers a good emotional response."

A salesman we know who is extremely successful at

establishing rapport with his customers, at creating a type of sexual chemistry that makes selling much easier, told us, "There is a moment in a sales pitch when an arm around the shoulder or a hand on the back will help swing the deal. It will project warmth and sincerity.

"But you must know that moment! Try it too soon and you kill the deal—too late and you've lost your opportunity. Too soon, it projects a falseness. The customer is going to think, 'Why is this character getting so chummy? What's he trying to put over on me?' and he's instantly wary about the whole deal."

In the same way, in a personal situation touch too soon can "freeze" the other person. Our friend, the woman who was so skillful at using touch in a social situation, was well aware of this. She used *accidental* touch—a brushed thigh, a hand touching the man's arm to steady herself as she reached over to the coffee table—the seemingly unconscious touches that have an equally unconscious effect. She used all of these at the beginning of any relationship.

The *deliberate* touch—her hand on a man's arm, or even his thigh—came later, after a sense of warmth and understanding had been created.

There is also the *healing* touch, which many parapsychologists believe to be a manifestation of the Kirlian effect. Semyon Davidovich Kirlian, a Russian, discovered this phenomenon in 1939, and it has been extensively investigated since, here and abroad. Under certain photographic conditions Kirlian was able to take pictures of an ordinarily invisible field, or aura, around any living object, plant or animal.

In some people the aura was mild. In others it projected some distance in flares of intense color. The aura could not be seen by the naked eye, but it showed up beautifully with Kirlian photography.

This aura, stronger in some people than in others, may not be visible, but there are many witnesses to the fact that it can be felt, and it may well be the source of the healing touch. There are people who have the ability to comfort, calm, and perhaps even heal with their touch. When someone with that ability touches you on the back with a friendly gesture, the reaction can be deep enough to stir your entire body and ignite a feeling of sexual chemistry.

A friend of ours went to a nude encounter weekend a while back, when such things were popular, and she said it taught her a great deal about herself. "But it also taught me about touching. There was one session in a darkened room where all of us, men and women, were told to move about touching each other—nothing more than touching. We were to let ourselves go, the instructor insisted, simply experience the touching.

"At first it was strange, disembodied hands against my body, my own hands touching others—and a mass of confused feelings within me, fear and tension and what-the-hell-am-I-doing-here—and then, without warning, there was one touch that was so different from all the others that it shocked me completely. In the dark, without knowing who it was, I felt an immediate response, and such a response! There was a sense of comfort and—yes, actual joy. I was left weak and shaking. I kept moving around the group trying to meet that touch again, and experience that same feeling."

"And did you?"

"Yes. And then, a day later, at dinner, when we were all dressed, one of the men I had barely noticed before put his hand on my arm, and suddenly I recognized that touch. I felt that same weakness go through me as I looked up at him. Till then he had been just one of the group, but I knew then I had to know him. I couldn't end the weekend unless I did.''

"What happened?''

"Well, it was certainly the start of something. We still see each other. But to me the wonder of it is that until I felt that isolated touch of his in the dark room, I didn't know how special he is, and if I hadn't felt that touch, maybe I'd never have known it.''

Not everyone has that unique and healing touch, but every one of us can use touch to convey a message of warmth and understanding, whether it's between the sexes or within one sex. A tremendously moving photograph taken on the battlefield during the Korean War shows a soldier holding another wounded soldier in his arms, and even the black-and-white picture conveys the sense of comfort and reassurance the touch of the soldier's arms gives to the wounded man.

Solace, comfort, reassurance, warmth, understanding, love, and attraction can all be signified with touch, and it is interesting to realize that our recognition of all this lies in the different uses our language makes of the word *touch*. We are touched when something moves us emotionally. A sad scene is touching, a gesture or an act can touch our heart—and all of it is a realization that touch is a supremely important element in our lives.

It becomes evident, then, that while sexual chemistry is an amalgam of many seemingly mysterious elements, most of them can be isolated and understood—and indeed used to create a situation in which sexual chemistry will operate more easily.

In this chapter we've covered the body-language elements: eye contact, nodding, posture, and touch. None of them are guarantees that an instant, or even a slow, attraction will take place, but without them there will be no attraction at all.

They serve as devices to get rid of the blocks that many of us put up unconsciously, blocks that prevent sexual chemistry from occurring. With all of them there is the element of internal feedback. Once we use a device to make us more open, more receptive to someone else, we begin to *feel* more open and receptive. This, in turn, makes it easier for us to act open and receptive.

It isn't quite a circle but more like a spiral, and it opens up as it progresses. Our personality, which originally prevented us from causing sexual chemistry to occur, gradually changes to the point where it actually invites sexual chemistry.

3
Metacommunication

LOVE AT FIRST SOUND

Some time ago one of us was a guest on a television program in Cleveland, and Julie London, the singer and actress, was another guest on the same program. We talked a bit while waiting in the Green Room and became quite friendly. A few weeks later, flipping the television dial, we heard Julie London delivering a commercial for a popular beauty product. The extremely sexy voice she used was not the voice of the woman in the Green Room—and yet it certainly was Julie London. Had her voice been dubbed?

No—it became apparent she had simply lowered her register, resonated from her chest instead of her head, and achieved a husky, sensuous quality—a quality clearly calculated to exert a sexual chemistry on any male viewer. This was slightly paradoxical, because the users of the beauty product were women.

However, advertising, in this area, often seems to

display this same paradox: a beautiful woman establishes a sexual chemistry with men to sell products designed for women, or a handsome man projects the same chemistry while huckstering a man's product. The answer, of course, is identification. Women identify with the sexy-voiced Julie London, just as men might identify with the handsome male model.

Watching Julie London led us to begin studying the vocal delivery of women news commentators on television, and it soon became apparent that those women who had managed to lower their registers and get rid of the nasal quality and high-pitched tones of their voices were more successful.

The voice has the power to communicate over and beyond the meaning of the words we use. A loud voice can signal any one of a number of things—anger, strength, authority, stress, fear—while a soft voice signals conspiracy, intimacy, secrecy, gentleness, or fear, too.

The words we speak have additional elements that shape and modulate them and add a tremendous amount to their meaning. It's not uncommon to have strong feelings for a disembodied voice; in fact, people have fallen in love with voices. A friend of ours, a ham radio enthusiast, told us that he met his wife by radio.

"She was from Nova Scotia and we met by ham radio. She was a bug about it too, and we'd talk half the night away. There was something about her voice—it always seemed to have a little laugh behind it, and she had that delightful Nova Scotian accent.

"Of course, there was the way she thought, too—we were both on the same wavelength—but in the final analysis it was her voice, soft, buttery, and with that little hint of amusement. 'This has to be one hell of a lady,' I decided, and on my next vacation I decided to go biking in Nova Scotia and meet her."

"And were you disappointed?"

"Not a bit. I was really in love before we met, and once we got together everything fell into place. We were married four months later."

The sexual chemistry between these two was ignited over a long distance without either seeing the other, and if we have any doubt that radio, projecting the voice alone, can do this, ask any popular radio figure how many marriage proposals he or she receives, how many effulgent fan letters, how many declarations of love. Indeed, sometimes the elimination of everything except the voice can make the sexual attraction stronger and more intense.

LET ME COUNT THE WAYS

Let's consider some of the ways in which the voice can carry its message. First of all, there is the emotional overlay. No matter what our words are, the emotion behind them carries a message. It can be harsh, gentle, raucous, pleasant, sarcastic, wheedling, whining, or any one of hundreds of others.

A friend with a daughter at college tells us that when she calls home he knows from the first two or three words whether or not there's a problem. "A whine usually means she's going to ask for money. A flat, depressed tone tells me things are going wrong with the boyfriend, a defensive note that she isn't doing well with her subjects.

A high, bright overlay says everything is fine. Her voice, no matter what she says, is the true barometer of her feelings.''

That overlay can also be the spark that ignites sexual chemistry in a new acquaintance. Take Allison. At a typical large cocktail party where everyone is sizing each other up, Allison selects her target for the evening, a man who appeals to her for one reason or another. She comes up to him and says, ''Hi. I'm Allison,'' and he looks up with quick interest, and you can see that something is starting to percolate.

Just what did Allison do to capture his attention so quickly? To begin with, her ''Hi'' was breathy, drawn out, almost two syllables, and it ended on a rising note, a bright sort of promise. Her ''Allison'' went down the scale, a warm announcement of her own identity. The three words are packaged in a complex manner, and there is a metameaning in them, a meaning above their actual meaning. *You interest me. We could have a good time together.*

In asnwer to Allison, the man she approaches says, ''Well, hello there!'' and the three words—the drawn-out ''Well,'' the upward inflection of ''hello there''—send out a message of pleased discovery. *How great to find someone like you!*

Every statement we make carries some sort of metameaning that adds a different dimension to our words. With the daughter calling home from college, it told what her real feelings were. With Allison, it was a heady promise of a lot of fun. With Elaine, a no-nonsense type at the same party, the message is very different. Elaine, when she meets someone, will say, ''Hi. I'm Elaine,'' but her ''Hi'' is short and direct, and ''I'm Elaine'' is a

statement of fact with no attendant frills. Her metamessage is straightforward—*Take me for what I'm worth*—with
no fancy promises.

Will Elaine's metacommunication start the same spark
that Allison's did? Only if the man she approaches happens to like straightforward women. But Elaine wouldn't
want any other kind of man, so her direct message serves
its purpose.

In turn he responds to her opening with "So you're
Elaine." It's said without the artificial inflection of the
man who responded to Allison. It's a simple acknowledg-
ment, but his choice of words gives what he says a sense
of appreciation, as if Elaine were someone he wanted to
meet, and it is also a reflection of her identity, an assurance that this will be a no-nonsense meeting. The
groundwork has been laid for sexual chemistry of a different sort.

These metamessages run through everything we say.
Listen to an adult talk to a baby and you realize that it's
less the sense of what's being said that's important than
the manner of saying it. Our voices usually change when
we talk to a very young child. Sometimes we lapse into
baby talk, meaningless syllables, or simply noises. The
words mean nothing at all; the metamessage in our
voices, the caressing and soothing sounds, penetrate to
the baby's consciousness.

But the metamessage in our voice works on adults, too.
How many husbands and wives go through the "I'm not
angry" routine while their voices drip with controlled
fury? And how many children pick up the annoyance and
distaste in their parents' voices during these "discus-
sions" that aren't really "fights"? "We never quarrel in
front of the children," but the children know. No matter

how neutral the words are, the packaging of the words comes out as cutting and cruel.

The packaging, the metacommunication, can be an emotional overlay, but it can also be a cultural bias. To an American, an accent different from his own can spell out a variety of things and send out a variety of messages. A young man who attended a coed camp when he was younger told us that he developed a terrible crush on a young lady because of her Southern accent. "It seemed so—well, sexy. That drawl caressed each word, and I used to get hot just thinking of her whispering sweet nothings to me. The hell of it all was that I discovered that she was no more Southern than I was. She had gone to a college down South for one semester and had come back with that sexy drawl. It didn't matter. I was ready to play along with her fantasy!"

The fantasy is what really affects any of us when we hear a regional or a foreign accent. This young man fantasized a Southern drawl as sexy. A young woman we know found a French accent exciting. "It just turns me on. I saw an old Charles Boyer movie on TV the other night, and I was just wiped out! And Belmondo! What he does to me . . ."

For others the turn-on is an Italian accent, or a Spanish one. Very rarely is a German accent considered sexy. It usually symbolizes humor, the crazy professor, the loony scientist. But of course there's always Marlene Dietrich. In the end, it's a combination of how the accent is delivered and your own inner world of fantasy.

A cultivated English accent can signal, among other things, intelligence and education. A businessman we know insists on hiring English women for receptionists. "They give the place class," he confided. "I've had customers tell me that a voice like that on the phone changed their entire attitude about the company.''

The accent in a voice can not only change one's attitude, it can also trigger release of the chemicals that buzz your brain, just as easily as a pretty or handsome face. A poll of American servicemen taken during World War II showed that among those who dated English girls, the accent was as strong a factor as any other single element in exciting their interest.

THE CHEMISTRY OF THE VOICE

There is more to a voice than a drawl or accent. Other elements send out equally powerful metamessages. The way we breathe, for example, has a lot to do with how others perceive us. When we're overcome by grief, fatigued, or depressed, we breathe shallowly, and this projects our true feelings. If we're angry or excited we breathe more deeply.

Our breathing affects the pattern of our voice, its speed and its vocal punctuation. Short pauses between our words give an impression of order. They tell the listener we're organized and definite. Too short a pause, however, sends a message of coldness.

The speed at which we speak sends another message. A fast talker can be persuasive; too fast and he becomes irritating. At the other end of the scale, a slow talker can signal conviction, thoughtfulness, and sincerity; too slow and he signals indifference. Our initial impression of another person is heavily influenced by the way he or she talks, the speed, and the pacing. One of President Carter's serious flaws in speaking was the way he paused. It

was not so much the length of the pauses as the inappropriate places he paused. This signaled confusion and
uncertainty—two qualities we abhor in a leader.

However, the type of pausing that in a public speaker
signifies uncertainty and confusion can, in an intimate
relationship, signal vulnerability. To the right person, at
the right time, this can be the right sexual chemistry.

One woman told us that she fell in love with her
husband the day he told her he was head-over-heels in
debt and just didn't know where to turn. "It was the
uncertainty in the way he said it, the odd, inappropriate
way he paused, that suddenly made me see this other side
of him, a weakness, an inability to handle things. You'd
think that would have turned me off, but actually it
suddenly made him more appealing, more human. Before that I always thought of him as the Rock of Gi-
braltar, able to handle any problem—and I found that a
little frightening. Now, to see him so completely bewildered did something, ignited some spark, and started
a real sexual chemistry between us!"

Another important element in speech is the rhythm we
use. When we first meet someone we usually ask, "How
are you?" and we stress "are." If we put the stress on
"how," we wouldn't make much sense. But if we stress
"you," the simple greeting becomes more intimate, and
the person being greeted becomes more interested.

The rhythm of speech—its stress and speed and the
pauses—spells out something about the speaker. If the
rhythm is good, our initial impression is pleasant, and the
possibility of sexual chemistry is much stronger.

Register and resonance in speech make another
strong impression on the listener. We noted, in the story
about Julie London, that lowering the register can make

a woman's voice sexy. How we resonate our voice has an equally strong effect. Women tend to resonate from the nasal spaces in the head, while men are more apt to resonate from the chest, for a deeper, stronger voice. In terms of metacommunication, that deeper resonance sounds more authoritative, more masculine.

"The first thing I noticed about Evan when I met him," a young woman told us, "was his voice. It was very deep and rich—a real man's voice—and somehow it turned me on. I hardly noticed his friend Paul. Paul had one of those nasal voices that just grated against my nerves. It seemed so—well, feminine or gay."

Unfortunately, this young woman made a bad choice. The deep resonance of Evan's voice gave the impression of strength. In fact, he was an emotionally shallow person, spoiled and unable to make a lasting commitment. "I'm sorry I passed Paul up," our friend admitted. "Now that I know them both, I really think he's much more of a man than Evan—but that's the way it goes."

"The way it goes" is that first impression, that first summing up of all the little elements that make sexual chemistry come into being. If, somewhere along the line, Paul had learned to speak differently, to resonate from his chest instead of his nose . . .

In addition to all the other elements that make up a voice—emotional overlay, resonance, speed, breathing, rhythm—there is volume. How loudly or softly do you speak?

Ellen was a soft talker. She had a pleasant voice, and there was rarely any trouble hearing her, but she spoke softly and with a certain intensity. "One of the things that first attracted me to Ellen," John told us, "was that soft voice. I come from a family of loudmouths. Mom shouts,

Dad shouts, my sister Marie shouts—and I find myself yelling as loud as the rest. Ellen, when I met her, was a shocker. I realized that with all the shouting we did at home, we never did any real listening.

"When Ellen spoke, I listened—just because of the softness of her voice. It caught me." He looked thoughtful, then added, "It's a funny thing about Ellen—not only do I listen to her, but I know she listens to me. She seems to focus in on what I'm saying. She makes eye contact with me, and her whole body seems open, receptive. The way she talks—well, there's a thoughtful quality to it that convinces me that she really wants to hear what I'm saying. You've no idea how important that is to me, coming from the type of family I have."

THE NAME'S THE GAME

There is another element that comes into play when we consider our voices and the messages they send. So far we've talked about the voice that projects the words, but we must consider the words as well. The words we choose have subtle meanings beyond their meaning. Simplicity is not very different from plainness in meaning, but the first sends a positive message, the second a negative. If we say a man has perseverance, we flatter him. Tell him he's stubborn and we put him down. If a woman is selective, it's admirable; if she's picky, it's irritating. A sensitive person is preferable to a touchy person, but both words can describe the same character trait.

"I think my moment of sexual chemistry with Claire came at a church social," Lenny told us. "I'm tall and too thin, and I've gone through life being called Skinny. I really hate it. My first acting role, in the second grade, was Jack Sprat in a production of Mother Goose stories. I cried the night before, all night, and I was too sick to go on the next day.

"Then, at the social, I was standing near the wall watching the dancers, and this girl comes up to me and says, 'Hi, Slim!' Goddamn, you could almost hear my heart pop! Slim! What a great name. Visions of cowpokes danced in my head. I asked her to dance, and that was it. We've been dating ever since."

Nicknames like Skinny and Slim carry their own meta-messages, but names also carry meanings. In a study of hundreds of names and what they suggested to people who heard them, Christopher P. Andersen, in his book *The Name Game,* found that all names suggest definite personalities. We tend to think of someone named Lana as alluring, Dotty as bouncy, John as a winner, and Kermit as unpopular.

Of course, the book was written before Kermit the Frog on the *Muppet Show* became a cult figure, and Kermit may no longer be an unpopular name. The popularity of names changes, and yesterday's loser may be today's winner. Browse through the current spate of romance novels and you'll find that the heroes' names run to Brad, Piers, Matthew, Ashley—names that the authors believe evoke a masculine image.

A different name can add a touch of romance, allure, and mystery to a person. Hollywood was well aware of this back in the thirties and forties, and when producers wanted to create a sexual chemistry between a star and an audience they changed the star's name to give it that extra metamessage. Frances Gumm became Judy Garland. Who on earth could relate to Gumm as the "girl next door"? Doris von Kappelhoff—imagine it on billboards—became Doris Day. Archibald Leach was renamed Cary Grant, Anna Italiano metamorphosed into Anne Bancroft, while Lucille le Sueur was too exotic an image for Joan Crawford, the twenties flapper, and Roy Scherer was too ethnic for Rock Hudson.

Today, a more sophisticated audience watching more realistic movies can accept an Al Pacino, Robert De Niro, George Segal, or Richard Dreyfuss without the glamour of a made-to-order name.

4
Of Pheromones and Fantasy

RAPED BY GYPSIES

"Did I ever tell you," Alan asked us, "about the time I was almost raped by gypsies?"

That grabbed us. "Come on now, you're kidding!"

"I'm dead serious. Actually, it was gypsy moths. We had a plague of them at our place in Connecticut, and I bought some of those traps that consist of a sex attractant in a plastic cage. The attractant lures the moths into the trap, and a killing fluid inside does the rest. I attached the attractant strips inside the plastic cages late one afternoon and hung them from the apple trees out behind our house. Then I started back through the dusk. What I didn't realize was that I had handled the attractant strips and the powerful chemical on it was all over my hands.

"Well, all at once the dusk around me was filled with the fluttering shapes of pale gypsy moths, their white wings beating against me as they settled around me like a cloud. I was charmed at first, because in the blue twilight

their lacy white shapes seemed ghostlike, sad, and somehow lonely—and then I suddenly realized that they were
all over my face as well. I must have rubbed my nose,
and they were actually clogging it up!

"Panic set in, and what had seemed beautiful was
suddenly deadly. I slammed at my head and body and
rubbed them off frantically. Perhaps there weren't as
many as I thought, but they seemed overwhelming, sti-
fling. When I finally got into the house, my wife helped
me pick the survivors off, and I was actually shaking."
He shook his head. "Believe me, it was a sexual attack!"

The attractant Alan told us about is the latest effort to
control the gypsy moth. It is an artificial duplicate of
something called a pheromone, a substance manufactured by female moths, irresistible to male moths. They
home in on it as if it were a sexual beacon, their little
antennas quivering. It's not a matter of choice. There is a
system in these insects that simply cannot resist the call of
the pheromone, and the smallest, almost microscopic
amount of pheromones can travel for miles, an un-
quenchable olfactory signal.

The word *pheromone* was borrowed from the Greek in
1959 by German researchers to describe this strong attractant. It means *to transfer excitement,* and that is exactly
what it does. Jean Henri Fabre, the great French natural-
ist, discovered insect sex attractants back in the early
1800s, but he simply described some of their actions
without exploring them deeply.

In the 1930s there were detailed studies of these strong
olfactory signalers as a way of controlling insect popula-
tions. Since it was tremendously difficult to gather natural attractants, artificial analogues were developed.

Not only moths, but ants, cockroaches, beetles, butter-
flies, and many other insect species rely on odor to com-

municate their readiness to mate. When the female insect is sexually ready, she sends out her unique pheromone and the males flock to her, sensing the pheromone with their antennas, often from miles away. It is sexual chemistry in the most basic sense of the word.

THE ANIMAL WORLD AND COPULIN

These irresistible odors that arouse the sexuality of the male, and in some cases the female, are not limited to the insect kingdom. Vertebrates, from fish to dogs, also rely on scent signals to mark territory, send out alarms, issue angry warnings, show aggression, and attract mates. Mice use their urine for sexual signaling. If a male mouse in a laboratory lets a few drops of his urine touch the cage floor, any female in a nearby cage will start her estrous cycle and become ready for mating. The signaling pheromone is in the urine, and the male mice can thus control the reproduction of the females.

Many other animals have the same sexual scent system, and the pheromone works both ways. In mice they ready the female for mating; in hamsters vaginal secretions with pheromones excite the males sexually. Cats, rabbits, sheep, goats, deer, and dogs all have different systems for scent signaling. All are turned on in one way or another by individual pheromones.

This sexual reaction to odor is so universal that farmers often use an aerosol product that contains an artificial sexual pheromone in order to ready a sow for artificial insemination. If the artificial pheromone is sprayed where the sow can smell it, she will at once assume a rigid posture that would enable an aroused boar to mount her.

The same rigid posture makes artificial insemination easier.

But as we rise higher in the animal world, pheromones, while still at work, become less important. In the primates the growing brain begins to fight the automatonlike behavior that pheromones arouse. Dr. Richard P. Michaels, a British psychiatrist, has studied odor reception in rhesus monkeys, and he has decided that vaginal odors play an important role in the sexual activity of the monkeys.

Dr. Michaels and his associates found a substance in the monkey vaginas that occurred in the middle of the estrous cycle, when the female monkey was sexually ready to mate, and had the ability to sexually arouse the male monkey. They named the substance copulin and concluded that it was a pheromone and was nature's way of turning on the males when the females were particularly fertile.

But are the same or similar pheromones present in human beings? That has been a question under scientific study for years without any definite answers, although the evidence seems to indicate that they are present, and they do work.

A friend of ours, a science-fiction writer, told us of a plot of his that involved pheromones. "I have this guy from today go back in a time machine to the Middle Ages, and the one thing that overwhelms him is the human odor. Nobody washed then, and at first he finds it horrible, but after a while he begins to get used to it, and then he begins to like it and react positively to it.

"My theory is that unwashed humans produce enormously powerful attractants, not only sexual, but on the level of friendship, aggression, and even hate. You just have to hate some people for their smell, while other smells make you love them.''

Our friend never did write his story, but his plot may have the answer to the argument about human pheromones. In today's Western culture—at least in America—we wash away every trace of odor from our bodies, and then we use deodorants to clean it even further.

Some years ago an extremely successful ad campaign for Lifebuoy soap invented "B.O." (body odor) as a tactic to urge people to buy their soap. B.O. was considered the very worst thing that could happen to you socially. Wash it all off!

But our society, so eager to sell through advertising, discovered that certain perfumes, when mixed with the natural pheromones of animals—musk from the musk deer, civet from the civet cat, and castoreum from the beaver—exerted a strong sexual attraction. The industry that had first urged us to wash off every trace of human pheromones now urged us to put on a perfume or toilet water laced with animal pheromones.

IT'S THE PITS

But even with this wash-and-perfume routine, the natural body odors do work through, and they do have an effect. Sara tells us she fell in love while dancing. "We had spent the night at a disco, my new friend Marty and I, dancing up a storm. For the first two hours I don't think either of us touched the other. It was the usual solitary dancing, and then, almost as a gag, they began a slow, old-fashioned number, 'Dancing in the Dark.'

Marty said, 'Come on. We'll do a little cheek-to-cheek.'

"We were both sweated up, and it wasn't really cheek-to-cheek. Marty's too tall for that. My nose came up to his armpit—and that's the point of it all. While we danced I suddenly smelled Marty. Now I know this sounds awful, but I was terribly excited sexually. How can I describe that odor? It was musky and soft and warm and so goddamn male! I couldn't wait to get Marty back to my apartment. It really turned me on!''

The odor that Sara and others as well described sent us to the medical library to see whether there was any difference between the odor of the armpit and that of the rest of the body. Not surprisingly, we found that there was. In addition to the usual eccrine glands, which secrete colorless sweat, the armpit has apocrine glands, which usually occur where there is hair. These glands secrete sebum that spreads out along the hairs. The hairs form a bigger area for evaporation, and the bacteria of the skin break the sebum down into a substance that gives off a musky odor.

Other body areas with the same type of glands are the scrotum and the base of the penis in men, and the skin around the vagina in women. In men and women the area around the nipples contains apocrine glands. The foreskin of the penis and the folds around the clitoris also produce secretions with a heavy odor, but these areas—the breasts, the ano-genital area, and the sexual organs—are usually protected by clothes. The armpits, not as closely covered, also sweat most easily, and the sweat accentuates that musky underarm odor.

In less deodorized cultures than ours the sexual attraction of the armpit odor is duly recognized. In Greece and some of the Balkan countries men carry handkerchiefs in their armpits during folk dances, and in the course of the dance they will offer these handkerchiefs to women to attract them as partners.

Richard von Krafft-Ebing, in one of his outrageous studies of Victorian sexual pathology, tells of a man who kept a handkerchief in his groin and used it to seduce women. They were unable to resist him once he brought the handkerchief to their faces—or it could be that the ripeness of it simply stunned them. Our modern culture shudders at the idea. "Incredibly raunchy," one woman told us, but with an intrigued shiver.

Perhaps the Victorian lady who dropped her handkerchief to attract an attentive male was aware of this sexually provocative glandular odor, for she often kept her handkerchief in her bodice. We find the male use of armpits and groin "extremely gross," but a feminine handkerchief from the same areas would seem rather exciting to most men.

There is, after all, a good reason why the sexual chemistry of odor should work. In an earlier section we told of the limbic region of the brain and its ability to be influenced by norepinephrine produced by the body. Primitive animals have a large area, the forebrain, devoted to the sense of smell. Our own cerebral cortex developed from this area. The limbic system of the brain has been traced back, in evolutionary terms, to the primitive forebrain, the area that responds to pheromones.

The limbic system in humans is the area responsible for pleasure, the area that contains the pleasure center and regulates sex drives and the reproductive cycle. Some of the nerves from the olfactory center in the nose go to the limbic system to stimulate its emotional and sexual center when the proper smell is released. Consider that this is also the center where norepinephrine works its magic and you can begin to see a close tie between odor and sexual chemistry.

THE ODOR OF THINGS PAST

The human sense of smell is inextricably linked to memory. There is a growing body of evidence that we remember what we smell longer than what we see or hear. Professor Trygg Engen of Brown University has done research that suggests that this persistence of memory is tied up "to a unique brain structure for olfactory processing," and he links norepinephrine to a perception of odors.

A link like this is also a link between smell and emotion and sexual chemistry. "I fell in love with my wife," Peter told us, "when I first took her out, and I can recall the exact moment. I picked her up in front of her house, and opened the car door to help her in. Then, when I climbed behind the wheel, I was suddenly overwhelmed by her perfume. It was Shalimar, a rich, vanillalike scent, and I had one of those intriguing moments of—well, I call it hedonic reaction.

"I was carried back to the last time I visited my aunt, a woman I loved dearly. She always wore Shalimar, and the scent of it was able to evoke everything about her. My aunt was everything feminine to me, alluring, lovely, gracious—a total woman—and there in the car I associated this new date of mine with all of those qualities. What else can I say? I fell in love!"

A young woman reported a similar experience with her boyfriend. "The first time he kissed me I smelled bay rum, an aftershave lotion, on his face. The odor was so strong and piercing, and so unusual. So few men use it, but my father did, and every time he picked me up I smelled that tangy odor. It started all those wonderful wheels of memory grinding, and I returned his kiss much more eagerly than I intended. I think that really turned him on, and now things are pretty serious between us.''

These two experiences are not isolated cases. Every one of us, at one time or another, has had the "hedonic reaction," that moment of exquisitely pleasant memory recalled by a scent. If the reaction occurs when we meet someone new, it acts as a type of bonding, shortening the "getting acquainted" time.

Dr. William S. Cain, an associate fellow of the John B. Pierce Laboratory and a professor at Yale University, believes the hedonic reaction is triggered by the olfactory neurons, which send messages to the olfactory bulbs, two lobes at the base of the brain. From these, the messages continue to those brain regions that take care of emotional responses.

Our culture has taught us that body odors are offensive, and cautions us to remove them all. But, because advertisers recognize the tremendous strength of smell in arousing sexual chemistry, we are then prodded into replacing the natural body odors with artificial scents.

That these artificial scents work is more a tribute to our olfactory makeup than to any innate condition of the perfume. We respond to odor, and that response is linked to emotion. If we are assured that the odor is sexual, as we believe perfumes are, we respond sexually. If we are taught that the odor is disgusting, as we are taught body odors are, we respond with distaste. That this is not a universally human response but a cultural one becomes evident when we realize that other societies respond positively to body odor, and even in our own society we react positively at a subconscious level. Without quite knowing why, we are attracted to someone because of his or her subtle odor.

Two researchers who are aware of the possible sexual attraction inherent in scent are William H. Masters and Virginia E. Johnson. In their book *Human Sexual Inadequacy* they stress the use of scents in their sex clinic. They incorporated the scents into a moisturizing lotion used for massage between a couple with sexual difficulties. The act of massage was an extended touching experience and helped break down sexual barriers within the relationship. One of the primary contributions made by these different scents, they noted, is "its stimulation of another of the major senses." They pointed out that the couples who enjoyed scented lotions believed that the use of fragrances carried erotic implications.

Their final conclusion from a pilot study of the use of different scents was that the sense of smell had a tremendous potential in the treatment of sexual dysfunction. It allowed patients to respond more easily, but since the different perfumes were used in massage lotions, we can't overlook the area of touch involved in the treatment. The combination of scent and massage is a heady experience. By stimulating the olfactory center under the erotic stimulus of touch, scents can evoke an emotional response, can, in fact, free a person to some degree and allow a natural chemistry to occur.

Masseurs are usually aware of this hedonic effect, and to avoid it they will use only unscented oils during massage. "Scented oils arouse my patients, men and women," a professional masseur told us. "I just can't handle that. I use a very light mineral oil, warmed up, and I don't allow scents anywhere in my studio!"

5

Love and the Amphetamines

"Do you know," Ken told us, "there was a time when I was hooked on speed—and falling in love with every girl I met!"

We couldn't believe it. Ken is your perfect image of the proper executive—almost fifty, married, and with two grown children, he's an account executive at a large advertising agency in New York, and he is the very model of your basic good citizen. Ken hooked on speed? Impossible.

"Well," he explained, "we didn't call it speed then. It was back in '56, and I was just a kid in my first job, writing copy for a big pharmaceutical house in Philadelphia, and we manufactured an amphetamine product.

"In those days amphetamines were the new big break-through in drugs, and we thought they were absolutely harmless. Working for the company, it was pretty easy to get as much as you wanted, and I used them all the time—to keep awake when I had an assignment to do at home, to stay alert when I was driving at night, to be bright-eyed and bushy-tailed when I came to work after a night on the town. We all figured it for a miracle drug, and none of us knew we'd get hooked.

"I'm not going to go into the rough part of the story, how I finally woke up to what was happening and kicked the habit. It was awful, but the point I want to make, the point that should interest you two, is that during the two years I was hooked on amphetamines, I was in and out of love a hundred times."

"You're exaggerating."

"I'm not. I'm honestly not. That drug did something to me. Somehow or other it stimulated an erotic side of my nature and I went crazy over almost every girl I met. It was this sexual chemistry you talk of, but over and over and over! I'd be high on the stuff, meet a girl at a dance or a friend's house, and wham! I was off. Then I'd come off my high a day later and wonder what I saw in her."

What Ken "saw" in those girls was something we put down to youth and a strong libido at first, but as we began to study the literature on sexual chemistry we realized that it was more than youthful ardor. Falling in love, that first excited flush that changes your entire outlook, that overwhelming attraction for another person, has to do with the stimulation of the brain by a chemical substance released by the body, most probably, according to researchers, phenylethylamine, a substance that acts in much the same way that the amphetamines do. Phenylethylamine, norepinephrine, and dopamine all have similar roles.

They cause our hearts to beat faster. They increase our energy and heighten our emotional outlook. They make us feel more optimistic, give us a better sense of ourselves—and make us more capable of falling in love. The seemingly trivial incident under normal conditions can trigger a sexual attraction under the heightened awareness of these substances—or of speed. Our friend Ken, high on amphetamines, was a sitting duck in every encounter with a woman.

What Ken experienced in his amphetamine highs, that constant sexual chemistry with every girl he met, may seem strange, but it bears out a theory of emotion put forth by Dr. Stanley Schachter in an article called "The Interaction of Cognitive and Physiological Determinants on Emotional State"—a mouthful of a title for an intriguing theory. Schachter believes that emotion involves two steps. First, the body is aroused physiologically by hormones or shock or drugs or even exercise. Second, we label this arousal according to social cues in our environment, our situation at the time it occurs. If the arousal occurs when we are watching a horror movie, we call it fear. If it occurs when someone is criticizing us, we call it shame. If it occurs in the presence of an attractive person of the opposite sex, we call it love.

If a young man, for example, is aroused by the exertion of a very physical dance, and his partner is an attractive young woman, sexual chemistry is likely to occur. If both partners are romantics, they will call it love. If they're more cynical, they'll label it a sexual attraction. If something goes wrong at that first meeting, the arousal can easily turn from attraction to dislike and even hate. The point is, both people are aroused, and there has to be a label for that arousal, whether it's love or hate or shame or fear.

A fascinating experiment was reported in the *Journal of Personality and Social Psychology* by three researchers, Drs. G. L. White, S. Fishbein, and I. Rutstein. They divided

a large group of men into four parts. One of the divisions
was read a very dull lecture on the anatomy of the frog.
The other three groups were put through experiences
calculated to arouse them. One group listened to a wild
and funny comic on a record, another to a gruesome
story of a murdered and mutilated missionary, and the
third group was simply asked to run in place for a few
minutes.

Afterwards, all of the young men were shown a videotape of an attractive young woman talking. When asked
if they'd like to date this woman and kiss her, the three
groups who had been shaken up by exercise, a comic
routine, or a horror story all responded more positively
than the men who had sat through the dull lecture on the
frog.

These studies added some validity to Ken's arousal by
amphetamine and his attraction to every pretty girl he
met. Fortunately for him in those years, the emotions he
felt were one-sided. The women he fell for were only
occasionally attracted to him in turn, and since his mini-
love affairs wore off as soon as the amphetamine did, he
could always look at his situation rationally and back out
of it gracefully.

Sexual chemistry, unlike sexual attraction, is a two-way
street. Both partners must feel it if it's going to work, and
there must be an interaction between the partners. Sexual
chemistry can be ignited by anything—a phrase, a touch,
a certain glance, a hat or a dress or a suit—but unless
there are continuing elements to feed that momentary
ignition it will fizzle out. For the chemical action to really
get under way, there must be a constant fueling of the
fire.

TURNED ON BY A JOKE

"I noticed Greg when he told a really involved joke about heaven and hell—really noticed him, that is," Gillian told us. "A group of us from the office had gone out for Chinese food, and Greg told this hilarious story with such a great delivery. It was an eye-opener for me, and I kept looking at him, and of course he noticed it and smiled back. I think it might have just stopped there, but later he told me that he couldn't get over my English accent, and he kept talking to me just to hear the way I sounded."

Greg, listening to Gillian, nodded. "At first it was her accent, but then she really has a great sense of humor, not just because she laughs at my jokes, but she comes out with those one-liners that just lay me flat."

That dinner at the Chinese restaurant was the start of their romance, Gillian and Greg told us, but the chemistry between them could have died that night if it weren't for the feedback of both their senses of humor. Humor was tremendously important to both of them. "I need someone who can pick up on a line and feed it back to me," Greg confessed, "and Gillian does just that. She's not only a funny lady but a fast one."

"We have our own type of shorthand," Gillian said. "It's like that old gag about the group of men who told the same jokes to each other so often they just had to call out the number of the joke, 2, 38, 71, and the rest would double up with laughter. Well, Greg and I are like that. A word now, even a gesture between us, can start both of us off, and it gets better. It sort of feeds on itself."

"At first," Greg said, "I was turned on by Gillian's

sense of humor, but then, as we began to go out with each
other, I started to find other things about her: the way she
dresses, the music she likes, her political views, the movies and books she likes—even her perfume. One thing
seems to lead to another."

"And it's the same way with Greg," Gillian admitted.
"The best way I can describe it is we mesh."

That meshing is what keeps sexual chemistry alive. A
marriage counselor we talked to likened it to magnetism.
"It's a magnetic quality that seems to pull two people
together," he told us. "It seems at its most obvious
between a man and a woman, but two women can feel it
for each other—or two men. When a politician or an
actor has it, we call it personal magnetism. That's just
another way of saying he attracts people, draws them to
him."

"But between a man and a woman," we asked him,
"how would you describe that magnetism?"

He shrugged. "How do you describe a force like that?
Physicists can't even define the physical magnetism we
see all around us. How can I describe this psychological
magnetism? Well, there's energy involved. Each partner
puts energy into the relationship, and each partner's
energy works on the other to draw out even more energy.
In true sexual chemistry, your partner will bring out the
best in you."

"Or the worst?" we asked.

He was thoughtful. "Yes, I suppose, for example, you
could say there was true sexual chemistry between Bon-
nie and Clyde, the famous gunman and his moll. And the
force between them, the magnetic strength of their relationship, caused them to murder and pillage. In a sense,
then, sexual chemistry brought out the worst. But if you

turn that around and look at it from another viewpoint, it was their best—their best at doing terrible things—and the truth of that lies in their enduring fame."

He hesitated. "You must understand, particularly if you're writing about sexual chemistry, that it can be the source of the most intense human pleasure. It's almost a mystical condition, a transcendental state. When you experience it, you believe you can do anything—there are no bounds or limits. That euphoric feeling, so typical of sexual chemistry, is often the downfall of the person who feels it."

"How is that?"

"Well, suppose, as often happens, sexual chemistry occurs between two people who shouldn't experience it— say, between a married man and someone else's wife. There are enormous difficulties in that sort of situation. A sensible person would consider the difficulties and decide to either give the other person up or carry on a very secret affair. But true sexual chemistry makes people careless in evaluating the pros and cons. The euphoria, the hedonic reaction, makes them certain they can handle it, and before you know it the two are plunged into bitter divorces, family messes, broken friendships. Do you know how strong you must be to withstand all that and still keep the chemistry alive?"

"But some people do."

"Oh, very few. Most, if they're carried away enough to try it, come out bitter, disillusioned, and with the bloom off the affair—a hell of a way to start a life together. I would advise two people like that who experience sexual chemistry but aren't entitled to it to forget it, or if they can't, to keep it secret."

He spread his hands. "You know, the society at large

recognizes this fact, and all sorts of labels are given to sexual chemistry when it occurs where it shouldn't. The favorite one is an *infatuation*. When a rich girl falls for a poor boy, her parents label it infatuation or puppy love. If both people are married to others, it's a *selfish passion*. Those two words carry a load of metacommunication! And, of course, if sexual chemistry occurs between two men or two women, it's *perverted love*, a *perverted attraction*, a *morbid fascination*."

"But there can be deep friendships with no sexual component between two people of the same sex."

"Of course. One of the important elements in sexual chemistry is that it can occur like that, within the sexes, and when it does and the two people are heterosexual, it's possible to keep the chemistry going and still function within society's guidelines. The sexual element is sublimated and turned into a deep friendship, sometimes into a teacher-mentor relationship. I've had people in every profession, actors, lawyers, doctors, tell me their most cherished moments were when they worked with someone where the chemistry was just right."

That magical moment can be witnessed onstage or in a motion picture when actors or actresses stir up just that perfect spark. Robert Redford and Paul Newman did it in *Butch Cassidy and the Sundance Kid,* and George Burns and Walter Matthau had it in *The Sunshine Boys.* Stan Laurel and Oliver Hardy and Bud Abbott and Lou Costello clicked perfectly in every comedy they made, and so did Dean Martin and Jerry Lewis, no matter how they got along offstage. Together, on the screen, there was a palpable chemistry. Two people, for one reason or another, worked smoothly together and created a certain feeling of excitement between them.

To find the same chemistry among women is more difficult. In the old *Mary Tyler Moore Show* it seemed to work with Valerie Harper as Rhoda and Mary, and in another TV sitcom Penny Marshall and Cindy Williams capture it as Laverne and Shirley. "But it's much more difficult to get that easy camaraderie among women," a feminist friend pointed out to us. "For too many years women have been pitted against each other. Another woman was always the competition even onstage or before a camera. The temptation is to steal a scene rather than to play off the other."

The same sort of sexual chemistry can occur between teacher and student. "I went through three years of high school learning only enough to get by," Eric, a writer, told us. "My teachers were symbols, figures of authority, and I fought them down the line, learning only the minimum I needed, and getting minimal grades. Then, in my senior year, I had Mr. Franklin for English, and the minute I walked into his class there was something between us.

"He wasn't very prepossessing, a short, balding man with tired, hooded eyes and a very cynical manner, but there was this instant attraction between us, and when he gave me back my first composition he looked me in the eye, a very piercing, direct look, and he said, 'I knew it as soon as I saw you. You've got something. This piece is good, but the next one is going to be better, isn't it?'

"I said, 'Yes,' hardly able to breathe, and believe me, my next composition was better, and every one after that was a shade better than the last. He didn't spare me. He ripped everything I wrote to shreds, but we both knew that was the only way. 'You're so far above the rest of the class,' he told me one afternoon when I had stayed after to get my paper back, 'that I'm not going to mark anything of yours. You'll get an A-plus in the course, but by God, you're going to write your guts out for me, aren't you?'

"I just nodded and laughed. That man woke me up, made me realize what I could do, not only in his course but in every other class I took. I never saw him after I graduated, and there was never anything personal between us, but there was a chemistry. When my first book was published I got a card from him. It said, 'Good!' That's all, but I treasured it over the best of my reviews."

THE SEXUAL ANORECTICS

One of the dangers of sexual chemistry is that people who experience it often fail to see either the true nature of their partner or the obstacles standing in their way. The literature of love is filled with irrational stories. People who experience sexual chemistry are often powerless to control their actions. They can be driven, perhaps possessed, to a certain extent mad. And a particularly pernicious condition exists when the object of someone's love cannot return what is offered.

One reason why this occurs, Helen Singer Kaplan, a New York City psychiatrist, explained to us, is because of a condition she labels *sexual anorexia*.

"A sexual anorectic," she explained, "is someone who doesn't feel the sexual urge. Infrequently it's due to a hormonal problem, but far more often it's rooted in a deep psychological conflict about love and sex."

We asked what could be done about it. "The most important aspect of sexual anorexia," she said, "is not what we do about it. That's for deep therapy. The problem most of us face in connection with sexual anorexia occurs when the irrational factor is so strong that we fall in love with a sexual anorectic.''

"But why would anyone be attracted to such a person? Why fall in love with someone incapable of returning that love?''

"There are the neurotic reasons," Dr. Kaplan answered, "wanting to hurt yourself, but there are also good, sound reasons. A sexual anorectic can still be physically attractive, beautiful or handsome, talented, bright and clever, have a marvelous sense of humor, be a good dresser—any of the things calculated to spark sexual chemistry. Once that's ignited, you tend to suspend all your negative perceptions and see only the positive side of the person.''

"What's the solution, then?''

"The solution, as always, is to face reality," Dr. Kaplan said. "That's the first step in solving the problem. Recognize the danger you are in, the one-sidedness of the situation.''

Thinking over what Dr. Kaplan had said, we were reminded of an interview we had with Steve. Steve met Lisa at a street fair in a large city. "A most unlikely place to pick up a girl," he told us. "She was in charge of a booth selling pottery. Lisa wasn't a potter, but her friend was, and she was helping out, and an attractive helpmate she was. She had long black hair and clear white skin and deep blue, almost violet eyes. She was wearing a long white dress with lace, and I took one look at her and lost my head. You've no idea how darling she was, like a character out of a Chekhov play.

"I bought two mugs and a casserole and three candle-sticks, and by then we were old friends, and I asked her out to dinner. She agreed, to my surprise. She was so pleasant, so—well, I guess you'd say passive, but we had a wonderful time, and it wasn't until I kissed her good night that I began to wonder. That kiss was like snow, cool and insubstantial. I saw her again, and again, and each time I enjoyed myself, but when I made any physical move she seemed to melt into herself. There was absolutely no response.

" 'What do you feel?' I asked her once, and she looked a little disturbed and shrugged. 'The same as anyone else.' But she didn't. There was no fire, no life behind that adorable facade. When I tried to push our physical involvement, to make love to her, she just seemed to fade away. It was less than resistance. It was nothing.

"We had a long talk, and I discovered that she had never been involved sexually—nor did she feel that she had missed anything. 'I like you, but I'm just not like that, Steve,' she told me. I tell you, it was heartbreaking. I was sure I could melt that block of ice she had for a heart, but I got absolutely nowhere. I wasted a whole month of my life on Lisa, and then I gave up. I don't believe anyone could have gotten to her."

That was Steve, a man who made an irrational choice, blinded by sexual chemistry, but knew enough to face reality, as Dr. Kaplan suggests. It was a wasted month, but only a month. Pamela, who ran into the same situation with Jerry, didn't have that much sense. Jerry, like Lisa, was a sexual anorectic. A handsome young man, bright and talented, he was wonderful company. Pam met him through a friend, and the two of them clicked in many ways. They made a perfect couple—as long as they kept out of bed.

"At first," Pam said, "I thought there was something wrong with me and that Jerry enjoyed my company but looked somewhere else for sex. Then I went through a period of thinking maybe he was gay, but I have some close friends who are gay and one of them met Jerry, and I asked him, frankly, what he thought. 'He's not gay,' my friend said definitely, 'but, Pam, you're wasting your time!'

" 'Do you think there's another woman?'

"He said, 'There's no one—not even you. Take an old buddy's advice and give it up. There's no future for you with Jerry. I've met his type.' "

But Pam couldn't give up. Sexual chemistry had made her illogical, and she was convinced that somehow, in some way, she could get through Jerry's defenses. What she didn't understand was that there were no defenses, just a lack of interest. It might have been just some wasted time, like Steve's wasted month with Lisa, but Pam went on for much longer than that. Unfortunately, Jerry satisfied a deep neurotic need in her. Being rejected, pursuing something that didn't exist, agreed with a sado-masochistic streak in her nature and drove her to keep on after Jerry.

In turn, he was not at all uncomfortable in the situation and was reluctant to break off. While he had no sexual interest in Pam—or in anyone else—he enjoyed her company, and his social life demanded a woman from time to time. Pam was perfect for that—and so the unhappy situation continued.

The cure, when dealing with a sexual anorectic, is two-part. First, you must recognize your partner for what he or she is, and second, you must get out of the situation as quickly as you can. You will probably be hurt, but the pain you feel now will offset a much greater pain in the future if you fail to end the relationship at once.

6
Image Projection

JEKYLL-AND-HYDING IT

"I lead a schizoid life," Brian told us. "I'm a sobersided minister by day and a bartender by night. If my nighttime self ran into my daytime one, I'm sure he'd back off."

"A minister by day and a bartender by night! All right, you'd better explain."

"It's simple enough. When we had our third child I knew my minister's salary wasn't enough. Either my wife had to get a job or I had to moonlight. The kids were too young for her to go to work, so I looked around for something—and I found a local restaurant and bar about twenty miles from our house."

"Isn't there a conflict of interest there, a minister and a bartender?"

"Not at all. I examined my heart very carefully—indeed, I prayed for guidance. I had to have another job, and this was available. It was nothing to be ashamed of."

"But tending bar . . ."

"It's far enough from my own parish so that I don't

run into any of my congregation, and I doubt if they'd recognize me anyway. The job has a sort of logic to it, for someone like me. As a minister, I listen to people's troubles and counsel them, and as a bartender I do the same thing." He laughed. "But you know, the funny thing about it is that I'm really two people, two different people. It's a kind of Jekyll-and-Hyde switch. With my collar on, I'm a serious character. People have confidence in me and trust me, and I respond to that.

"But at night I wear an open shirt without a tie and with my sleeves rolled up, and I'm a different person, the kind of guy you can relax with, easygoing, talkative, and I feel different. Really different."

When Brian changed clothes, there was a reinterpretation of himself. He saw himself differently, and acted differently. The casual life of a bartender gave him the right to be free and easy. All of us can adopt a different, perhaps a freer persona in one lifestyle than in another. When Brian dressed as a bartender he felt livelier, better able to extend himself, less confined than he felt dressed as a minister.

Brian's double personality, no matter what he thinks, isn't that uncommon. But there have to be two Brians for this double life to work, and as we talked to him it became obvious that there were indeed two strong and different sides to his character.

In the Jekyll-and-Hyde story, Robert Louis Stevenson had his good doctor discover a potion that released the dark side of his nature and gave it the upper hand. Stevenson's premise was that each of us has a good and bad side to us and one dominates the other. The good Dr. Jekyll had it all his way until the evil Mr. Hyde was released.

In Brian's case, there is nothing schizoid about him.

He is an excellent minister who takes his work and role seriously. As a bartender he can leave the "mentor" image behind, roll up his sleeves, and go to work. His magic potion is a change of clothes, as simple as that. This personality change with different clothes, with a different *image,* can happen to any one of us. Put your most staid businessman into a clown suit for a kiddies' benefit and watch the personality change. Dress your blue-collar worker in a well-fitting, very expensive suit with the accoutrements to match and he'll feel experienced and confident, a man of the world. Put any woman in a beautiful dress and she'll feel more attractive—and often she'll *be* more attractive. It's not so much a case of clothes making the person as it is of the person being aware of the image he or she projects in those clothes, and thus the statement he or she makes.

How many city men in sheepskin jacket, jeans, cowboy hat, and Western boots project a cowboy image though they would be terrified to ride a horse? And how many women in leather pants and high heels project an image completely at odds with themselves? Is the image what they would like to be, or is it one calculated to attract the other sex? Does the image project fantasy or reality?

Often it is fantasy, but in sexual chemistry fantasy can be as important as, or more important than, reality. To discover how men responded to an image of a woman without knowing what she was really like, a university study in Indianapolis had a young woman in a revealing tube top and short skirt ask directions from middle-aged men passing by. Later she changed to a tailored suit that was rather severe and repeated her request for directions.

In the revealing outfit she received help 70 percent of the time, in the tailored suit only 40 percent.

The clothes you wear create a persona that reflects in part your inner needs and in part how you wish to be seen. They also decide how others will see you. "It's a funny thing about my two selves," Brian told us. "As a bartender there's a certain amount of this sexual chemistry that goes on between me and the women at the bar. Oh, I never let it get overt, but I know it's there. There's a look in the eye, that certain smile—if I were that kind of man it could easily develop into something. As it is, I've learned very quickly how to turn it off. I have to, but I tell you, temptation is as close as the next drink I serve!"

PROJECTING A FANTASY

To gain some understanding of how we react to people's images, we talked to Dr. Avodah K. Offit, a psychiatrist and sex therapist affiliated with Lenox Hill Hospital. Dr. Offit has written two books on sex, *The Sexual Self* and *Night Thoughts*. "How important is image projection in creating sexual chemistry?" we asked her.

"We all make statements about ourselves which may or may not attract others," Dr. Offit said. "One man may wear a sweater and a beard with corduroy slacks and project the image of the intellectual writer. He's going to attract a woman who fancies the creative type. Remember now, we're talking about initial attraction, the spark that ignites that first moment and decides whether there is to be any interest or not."

"I can understand the intellectual or creative image, or a businessman's image, something logical, but what about your urban cowboy type? Can there be any appeal there outside of . . . well, a giggle at the incongruity of it?"

"You're not thinking broadly. The urban cowboy with his Western image can certainly turn women on. Think of what happens when you look at a painting. You ask yourself, 'What is this piece of work saying?' When a woman looks at a man in Western garb, the thing you must ask is 'What is his image saying to her?'

"In most cases it says, *I'm the lone hero*. She's seen enough westerns to understand the fantasy. It runs like this: *I ride the range alone and lonely. I'm self-sufficient and I can protect you against danger. I capture wild horses and tame them, and I can handle any ornery woman without trouble.* Now get the subtlety behind the fantasy. She can play at being the hard-to-get ornery woman, while he plays at the lone hero."

"Is it all a matter of fantasy?"

"What's wrong with fantasy? The bearded-and-sweatered type may never have written a word, the man with the business suit may work on the assembly line, but they are projecting fantasies too. So is the woman in the long white summer dress at the lawn party and the one in hot pants at the local disco. Remember back in the seventies when *natural* and *organic* were the buzzwords? Remember the girls in their long pioneer dresses? Whose fantasy were they fulfilling?

"Your urban cowboy either excites a woman or turns her off. Some women feel threatened by the 'lone rider' fantasy. He may symbolize a quiet menace that she isn't prepared to handle."

"Wouldn't most women see through it all?"

"Seeing through it is one thing. Preserving the fantasy is another. Let me tell you about an incident that happened in the park the other day. I was sitting on a bench when a young woman came toward me. She was wearing a highly styled silk dress and heels, and she had perfectly coiffed hair.

"Behind her there was another young woman in shorts and running shoes. She wore an old sweat shirt with a towel around her neck, and her face was covered with sweat. I could almost smell her from where I sat, that good, earthy smell of someone who's just had a real workout.

"A young man in jeans, T-shirt, and worn sneakers came toward the two women. His eyes flicked off the well-dressed young woman indifferently, but at the sight of the athletic girl behind her they lit up, and I could see sexual chemistry at work!

"He went a few steps past, hesitated, then came back and fell into step beside her as he started one of those pickup routines that are as old as Adam.

"What fascinated me was his complete lack of interest in the well-dressed young woman and his immediate response to the runner. Each was projecting an image, but obviously the image that interested him was the one he was most comfortable with. The runner matched some fantasy of his own—sports, health, a natural look, whatever."

THE BEAUTIFUL PEOPLE

Is beauty in women or handsomeness in men the primary spark that ignites sexual chemistry? Do good-looking people have an advantage over plain or ugly people in the sex game?

There is evidence that they do, and not only in the sex game but in all of life. There is a genuine prejudice in favor of attractive people. In an article on physical attractiveness in the *Journal of Personality and Social Psychology*, Dr. Karen Dion and her associates at the Universities of Minnesota and Wisconsin reported that they had prepared photographs of attractive people, average-looking people, and unattractive people and had shown them to a large group of men and women. They asked the group to rate the photographs in terms of personality.

The attractive people in the photographs were seen as more sexually warm and responsive, more sensitive, kinder, stronger, more interesting, poised, modest, social, and outgoing. They would get better jobs, make better husbands and wives, and they'd have happier marriages; in all these things, the judges decided, they'd do better than the plain or ugly people.

The conclusion is that most of us see good-looking men and women as more desirable and more interesting. They are, in short, more likely to start sexual chemistry going. With this in mind, it becomes obvious why all of us try to project the image we see as better-looking and more attractive.

Dr. Dion has explored another angle of the perception of beauty. She found that linking beauty to goodness starts back in childhood. We tend to judge children's behavior by their appearance. If a child is attractive, we are more lenient with him or her than if the child is ugly. We make excuses for beautiful children, forgive them more easily, and have greater expectations for them.

The children themselves are brainwashed very early on

with fairy tales about the beautiful good princess and the ugly witch, Cinderella and her ugly sisters. Good is beautiful, bad is ugly.

A friend of ours, a lawyer, told us that these expectations and the tendency to forgive attractive people reach into the courtroom as well. "I've done no exact study on it," he said, "and I can't quote you facts and figures, but I know and my colleagues know that juries are softer on good-looking criminals, and even judges tend to favor them.

"It's the image that matters. I dress my clients carefully in modest clothes, but never shabby. Solid-colored suits and white shirts and small-patterned ties for the men. Haircuts and shaves are mandatory, and I try to get them to shave off mustaches and beards. My women clients are told to wear simple dresses in dark colors with high necks and long sleeves, simple hairdos, and a minimum of makeup and jewelry. I know it sounds crazy, but the jury is going to base at least 50 percent of their judgment on how my client looks, not on what he or she says or did. It's appearance that counts, and if my client is handsome or pretty, I'm halfway home free."

He hesitated a moment. "One warning—you mustn't confuse sexiness with attractiveness. Blatant sexiness can turn a jury off, and, of course, there's one type of case where an unattractive person comes out ahead—that's any kind of con job. If the jury believes that the defendant took advantage of his God-given looks to sucker in a victim, they'll turn against him."

Research that suggests that our lawyer friend might be right comes from a study by Harold Sigall and Nancy Ostrove at Maryland University. They gave a number of students a story about a crime and asked how they would punish the offender. Some were given a photograph of a very attractive woman and told she was the perpetrator, while another group was shown a picture of the same woman made up to appear very unattractive. A third group was shown no picture at all.

Predictably, although punishments suggested for the unattractive woman and the woman of unknown appearance were very similar, the punishment for the attractive woman was much lighter.

Two conclusions come out of this study: attractive people can get away with a lot more than unattractive ones, and—and this is most important—the same person can affect us positively or negatively by changing her appearance. The woman who made herself attractive with cosmetics, hair styling, and facial expression stood a better chance than when she allowed herself to be unattractive.

It is not so much the appearance that nature gave us that counts either in getting on in the world or in creating sexual chemistry, but what we do with those looks, how we dress, how we cut our hair, how we make up if we are women, and above all how we compose our features. A simple smile can do wonders in projecting a favorable image. A sullen look can lose points.

When we approached Dr. Offit with this finding, she said, "All that may be true, but attractiveness is a very subjective thing. What one person finds attractive another may find boring. Before you can draw conclusions you must investigate attractiveness more closely."

But attractiveness, as we found out, is easier to recognize than to describe. Blond hair may be attractive where most people are brunettes. In Latin America it's high on the beauty list, but in the Scandinavian countries, where blonds are common, dark hair rates a second look, and dark-skinned people find themselves very popular.

But these things aside, most people can agree on what is attractive and what isn't. We found that out when we approached a large group of friends with twenty pictures of what we considered attractive and unattractive people. With only slight variations, our friends agreed with us and with each other, and whether they were men or women, their judgment of facial beauty seemed the same.

But the same uniformity of judgment doesn't exist when living people are used instead of photographs. Other factors come into play then: how a person holds himself, how mobile or stiff a face may be, a tendency to frown or smile. This was brought home recently when one of us was showing a friend pictures in an old school yearbook.

I came to a picture of Stella Gianetti, and I said, "Now there was a beauty! I think Stella was the most attractive girl in the school."

My friend studied the picture for a few minutes, then looked at me in bewilderment. "Either your memory is going bad, and it was another girl, or your judgment stinks. Take another look."

I did, frowning, and I realized that the girl in the picture wasn't at all good-looking. Her teeth were all wrong, and her nose was too long, and her lips . . . But I could close my eyes and remember Stella walking down the front steps of the school, holding her books to her, her head tall, her slim body held beautifully erect—and that dazzling smile of hers! "It's not that Stella was actually pretty," I tried to explain to my friend, "but it was everything about her, the confidence she felt in her own appearance, and the way she radiated that confidence, her walk, her speech—everything." I looked at the picture again and shook my head. "No picture could do her justice. A photographer just can't capture the quality Stella had!"

HENRY'S HEAVY HEARTBREAK TECHNIQUE

Henry, a young man who was not exceptionally attractive, told us he had a surefire technique with women based on a peculiar paradox of self-esteem. "When I first meet them, I treat them almost with contempt. I'm rude. I never try to flatter them, and I act indifferent, no matter what they're like."

"Does that ever get you anywhere?" we asked in surprise.

"It's the first step in what I call Henry's heavy heartbreak technique. The next time I meet them I'm much nicer, and the third time I fall all over them, and brother, it works! By the third date they're ready to go for broke. I don't know why it works, but it does."

The *why* in Henry's heavy heartbreak technique can be found in a study done by Drs. Elliot Aronson and Darwyn Linden and reported in the *Journal of Experimental Social Psychology*. They compared the effects of being consistently nice to people with being consistently nasty, and also with changing from nasty to nice and nice to nasty.

They found that someone who was always nice could generate a reasonable amount of sexual chemistry, and of course nice people who became nasty generated the least amount. But when you changed from nasty to nice the sexual chemistry was much better than when people were nice to begin with! Henry had chanced upon a basic truth: the people we like most are those we can convince of our own worth. If they are indifferent to us when we first meet them and then get to like us as they come to know us better, it convinces us that we have the power to influence them. If their appreciation of us comes slowly, it's bound to be a true realization of our worth. It's extremely flattering to convert someone into liking us, more flattering than to be seen as attractive from the beginning—and more likely to create sexual chemistry.

Diane used this technique without realizing it. "I think it's a matter of how I was brought up," she told us. "We were not a demonstrative family, and we held back on affection until we were sure someone had earned it. I carried that same approach over to the men I met—and the funny thing is, it seems to work."

Diane met Luke at a concert. "He was with some friends, and I realized that he kept looking at me, then avoiding my eye when I turned toward him. When we were introduced at intermission I was very cool, very distant, even though he really interested me. But I had heard stories about him from my friends—a real heartbreaker, they told me, watch out!—and I was very cagey the first time we met."

"I liked Diane's looks." Luke grinned. "And when she said, 'Oh, I've heard about you,' in that cold way she has, I became very curious. I might not have gone after her at first. She was so distant, disinterested. I'm used to women coming on strong, but that 'I've heard about you' was like a challenge, and I called her a few days later for a date. She agreed reluctantly, but warmed up during the evening, and I figured, aha, the old charm is working.

"By our third date she was her own self, warm, funny, and, what really mattered, I figured that I was the one who had turned her on. I'd won her over. I think that's what started the sexual chemistry between us, and then . . ." He shrugged. "It's been going on ever since."

What Diane had done, unwittingly, was bolster Luke's sexual self-esteem. The man who can thaw out the ice queen has to be a bit more of a man than anyone else!

Dr. Bernard Murstein of Connecticut College tried to find out how sexual self-esteem affects us when it comes to choosing a lover or mate. He tested about one hundred engaged couples and had them fill out a personality questionnaire in four different ways: one for themselves as they really were, a second as they would like to be, a third as they believed their lover was, and a fourth as they would like an ideal lover to be.

How much sexual self-esteem they had was decoded as the difference between the person's real self and ideal self. They concluded that people with high sexual self-esteem attract lovers closer to their ideal than do people with low sexual self-esteem.

A high degree of sexual self-esteem and a firm conviction of your own sexual identity are both necessary in creating sexual chemistry.

TURN-ONS AND TURN-OFFS

No matter how secure you are, no matter how strong your sexual self-esteem is, you must still put forth the right image if you wish to attract others and generate sexual chemistry. Ben, young and single, told us he had just about given up on parties and bars. "I feel pretty good about myself, and I used to try my damndest to make an impression when I went out. I would dress fit to kill, suit, tie, shirt. I'd walk into a bar—and I'd be ignored. It was humiliating, and finally I said, who the hell needs this? and I just stopped going to bars, and to parties, too.

"Then one night I was out for a walk in jeans and an old sport jacket and I passed one of the trendier singles bars downtown. I felt like a drink, but I hesitated about going in dressed like that. Then I said, to hell with it, no one is going to notice me anyway, and I walked in. Right—you guessed it. All of a sudden a woman was talking to me. It was natural, friendly, open. I thought at first it was that particular bar, but then I realized that it wasn't the bar at all. It was the casual way I was dressed. I belonged. I had been just too formal before, and I don't know why I never noticed it. Dressing like that had turned off the women I met."

With Ben's experience in mind, we asked a number of young men and women to talk to us about what they felt were turn-ons and turn-offs in the other sex.

The women and men were all single, the women in their late twenties, the men in their early thirties. We talked to each group separately to avoid their influencing each other. The first thing we discussed with the women was male attractiveness. "What do you find attractive in men? What do you find unattractive? What turns you on? What turns you off?

The social scene for these young people seemed to a large extent to revolve around singles bars, that vast arena where men and women can meet without obligations and, if desired, without carrying the acquaintanceship beyond the doors of the bar.

"I'm turned off," one young woman said emphatically, "by the strong come-on, the prepared line, the fast approach." The others agreed. "We like a man who is casual, who looks contented just being there. This goes for parties or bars—any kind of get-together. We like someone who talks easily to the bartender or host, who seems comfortable in the situation."

"What I can't stand," another said, "is the man who's always 'working the room'—someone with a roving eye while he's talking to you, a guy who scopes out the place. In fact, the opposite, a man who looks just at you, is very much of a turn-on."

"I don't like a glum man," a young woman offered. "There is nothing worse at a bar or party or any get-together than the man who sits there without a smile. I know that a lot of men consider it real cool not to show any emotion, but they don't realize how unappetizingly they come across. It's doom and gloom, and who needs it? Give me a smiler any day."

When the men were asked what makes a woman attractive, about one third answered in terms of themselves. "I like to feel she's attracted to me, that she wants to get to know me." "I want an attentive woman, someone who lets me know I turn her on." "I like someone who's interested in me, who wants to hear about me."

Another third reacted in terms of physical features. The women seemed more concerned about how the men acted, the men about how the women looked. "I'm attracted by her face and figure." "I like a woman who's built." "Her physical appearance."

The last third talked of personality, humor, intelligence, sensitivity. They liked women who were informal, at ease, low-keyed.

The women tended to react to men's clothes. None of

them liked what they called "the corporate look," men who wore a vested business suit with a tie to a bar. "Too neat. Belongs in the office. If they must come from work, let them at least take off the vest and tie and loosen the collar."

They liked men in jeans with sport jackets and sweaters. "Shoes are a real giveaway," one said. "No wing tips. Laced shoes if they're casual. Loafers—even running shoes." "Boots are okay," another decided. "Cowboy boots, sure, but short boots are out."

Another said, "What the men wear can be a little different, but not outlandish. I like a scarf over a jacket, but not a garish one."

They put emphasis on what a man carried as a prop. Most were turned on by a gym bag. "It shows he's athletic and healthy." Athletic and healthy were important considerations. "No cigarettes. They're disgusting and unhealthy." "If he absolutely must smoke, a pipe is okay, and on rare occasions a small cigar."

What came across as we talked was that "being healthy" was equated with animation, with liveliness, with using your body and face in an encounter, with showing emotion and humor. Done properly, this can turn a plain person into an attractive one.

Animated, healthy people have a sense of involvement, and while a prop like a gym bag is no guarantee that sexual chemistry will occur, it can be a conversation piece and offer an opportunity to talk about sports or any other activity. Behind the use of such a prop is the fact that it gives two people who meet as casually as this an opportunity to focus on something besides sex. It defuses the tension of a sexual encounter and, paradoxically, gives sexual chemistry a chance to develop.

All of the men disliked women who smoked. They

accepted drinking in a woman as long as it was "social."
But the women were selective about drinking men.
"Hard liquor is unhealthy too," they all felt, and agreed
that the most attractive drink a man could order was
imported beer. White wine was too effeminate, and
brandy in a snifter "too affected."

Jewelry worn by a man was a turn-off, the women
decided, and all of them detested gold chains. The men,
on the other hand, liked a woman to wear jewelry, "But it
mustn't be overdone." Some felt makeup should be moderate or nonexistent, but an equal number liked makeup
applied with taste. "It shouldn't distort a woman's looks.
It should improve them."

As far as the women were concerned, beards and
mustaches were popular. They liked men's hair kempt,
and they accepted baldness. But as one put it, "I just
can't stomach the bald man who combs what hair he has
left all the way over to one side. If he's bald, let him make
the most of it. Baldness can be sexy too. Look at Telly
Savalas and Yul Brynner."

Most men like women's hair to look natural, not obviously bleached or colored. "Hair that flows," as one
put it, and most of them liked women with long hair and
disliked short, frizzled cuts. Only a few of the men preferred blonds, putting an old wives' tale to rest.

The women wanted a "thinking man," but not a
phony. Flattery turned the women off, and they preferred
men with no obvious lines. They liked a man to zero in
on something obvious but true: "You have nice eyes" or
"I like your smile." It had to be something a woman
could believe and something that proved the man was
really seeing her as a person.

The men liked women to be light and engaging,

friendly without being aggressive or shy. They wanted a woman who could make them feel at ease without "pumping" them for information.

What seemed to come out of the session for both men and women was the fact that sexual chemistry occurred most easily with a partner who was natural and easygoing, somewhat laid back, a partner who wouldn't make too many demands, who was fairly conservative in dress but attractive. Feminine if a woman, and manly without being macho if a man.

The things that turned both sexes off and made sexual chemistry difficult were things out of the ordinary, too calculated, or loud. With both men and women, there was the paradox of wanting someone who stood out and yet fit in; someone special but familiar; someone sensitive and caring of others, yet aware of his or her own sexual self and with enough self-esteem to know his or her own needs.

The men were concerned with the way a woman looked, whether she was pretty and had a good figure. The women were less concerned with looks. They believed that sexual chemistry could occur no matter what the man looked like as long as he was dressed appropriately and exuded a sense of self.

7
Risking

STRENGTHENING YOUR SELF

While there is a great deal of agreement among men and women, old and young, rich and poor as to what is attractive in someone else, there is very little agreement about what is attractive in ourselves. We do not see ourselves as others see us. We gloss over our faults just as we gloss over our good points. The problem is, we know ourselves too well, and we allow that self-knowledge to influence our judgment.

In a doctoral thesis for West Virginia University, Norman Cavior discovered that three quarters of a group of schoolgirls thought that they were the least attractive girls in their class. As a rule, Cavior concluded, girls are so obsessed with the little things wrong with themselves that they fail to see what's equally wrong with everyone else.

And when little girls grow up, they aren't much different. Compliment your average women on her hair or her dress, and she'll almost automatically find some way to put herself down. "My hair needs washing—I was going to have it set." "Oh, this old thing? It's been in the closet for years."

Can you strengthen your own self-image? Are there ways of developing a stronger self? Or are we all doomed to go through life with the same self-image we have now?

Yes to the first two questions, and no to the third. We can change our self-image, and there are many ways to do it. One way is through the feedback method of body language. All of us have a body language that matches our personality. You can tell a timid, uncertain person by the hesitant way he acts, a depressed person by his slumping posture, and a self-assured one by the way she carries herself, the fact that she sits in an open, receptive position, makes eye contact readily, and is quick to smile, unafraid of showing emotion.

If you wish to strengthen your own self-image, you can imitate the body language of a self-confident person. If you do this often enough, you begin to feel more self-confident, more sure of yourself, and in turn that allows you to act self-confident more easily. A feedback mechanism is started, whereby the posture you assume affects your personality, and your personality in turn affects your posture.

At first you are only pretending to be self-confident, but after a while it is less and less pretense and more and more a permanent change toward self-confidence. The change is small at first, but it is constant, and if you keep it up over a long period of time your inner self will become stronger and more assured. Psychologists have used the method successfully to treat depressed patients as well as patients who hold themselves in low esteem.

There are other ways of strengthening your inner self,

and one of the most successful is risking. Bart is a classic example of someone who had a problem with risking, with taking a chance. Not in business, because he was doing well in his profession, but on a personal level.

"Right now I have a problem with Margo," he told us. "I met her while I was out jogging. We both hit the track behind the high school each morning at the same time, and we'd talk to each other as we ran.

"There was something about Margo that turned me on from the moment I met her. That wild red hair of hers—and her fantastic stride . . . Anyway, I'm dying to go out with her, but I just can't get up the nerve to ask her."

"But why not?" we asked. "What's the worst that can happen? You ask her and she says no. Is that so bad?"

Bart looked uneasy. "If she turned me down I'd feel too humiliated to see her again."

"Come on, it's not the end of the world."

"But why take a chance? As it is, we have fun running. If I ask her out and she says no, everything will be different."

In any kind of risk, the fear of rejection is a powerful obstacle. Bart, in his early twenties, had gone through life afraid to take a chance that would leave him vulnerable, open to rejection. After talking to us, Bart finally summoned up enough courage to risk asking Margo for a date—and to his dismay she did turn him down, gracefully, but still it was a rejection.

"I thought I would die," Bart said. "I felt so humiliated, so crushed. I had offered something and had been refused. I spent a miserable week. In fact, I went to the track an hour earlier each day just to avoid Margo—and that's how I met Shelly."

Shelly was a runner too, a bright, witty woman who liked the same things Bart did, who worked in the same field, and was, like Bart, a trivia freak. They began by trading trivia as they ran. "When I found out she knew all four countries in the Land of Oz, I fell in love with her," Bart told us. "But there it was. Did I dare take a chance and ask her out? Especially after the terrible experience I had had with Margo. But then I asked myself, how terrible was it? I survived, and I feel just as excited about Shelly as I was about Margo—more so. So I asked her out and she said sure, and tonight's the night!"

What Bart learned was that you can survive rejection and still live a full, normal life. The chances were pretty good that Shelly wouldn't reject him. How many men know the names of all seven dwarfs? But even if she did, he knew he'd survive.

YOUR RISK FACTOR

Some time ago there was a biography published of Dr. Harry Lorber, a well-known obstetrician who, at eighty-one, was still single. When he was asked why he had never married, he said, "Because I couldn't ever bear the idea of loving someone and then losing her. Suppose I committed myself to a woman and married her. Eventually I might run the risk of losing her through death or desertion. I couldn't stand that!"

It was amazing and sad that so intelligent and talented a man had gone through life alone and lonely rather than risk commitment and love. In some ways it was like the person who commits suicide because he can't stand the thought of dying, or the writer who can't bear to publish because the critics might destroy him, or the artist afraid to continue painting because he'll never reach the heights others have reached.

Fear of risking can only lead to stagnation and a dead end. Most of us go through life adding up the advantages and disadvantages of a situation, and then deciding whether it's worth taking a chance. Our inner *risk factor* is usually strong enough to allow us to take a chance if the goal is worth it. But there are many people who are terrified of any risk, and others who can risk things only after a great deal of inner turmoil.

How can you discover your own inner risk factor and decide whether it's strong enough or whether you need to strengthen it? It can be done by evaluating just how often you take risks. How easy is it for you to take a chance, or how terribly hard is it to make a decision?

There is a spectrum of risk, from the arrant gambler at one end, who will take a chance at anything, to the frightened introvert at the other end, who will risk nothing. If an honest self-evaluation is too difficult, the following test will give you a good idea of your own inner risk factor. There are ten situations presented here, and each one has three possible courses of action. Read each situation carefully and then decide which of the three solutions, A, B, or C, is closest to what you would normally do.

It is important that you answer with complete honesty and put aside all questions or morality, of right or wrong. Forget about the right answer. There is none. Concentrate only on what *you* would do. No one but you will judge your answer, and after all, the only risk you'll be taking is the risk of better understanding yourself.

▶ 1. You are a woman and on impulse you buy a
        revealing slit skirt, or you are a man and on
        impulse you buy an avant-garde shirt.

   A. You decide to wear the skirt/shirt to work.

   B. You won't wear it to work, but you will wear
        it out on a date.

   C. You return it the next day and wonder what
        on earth impelled you to buy it in the first
        place.

▶ 2. You meet a stranger on a plane and he/she is
        attractive, but you know nothing about him/her.
        He/she suggests that the two of you have dinner
        together that night.

   A. Sure. You like him/her and it might be fun.

   B. You suggest a foursome with a couple you
        know.

   C. Absolutely not.

▶ 3. You are at an intimate dinner, and at the table
        someone mentions a playwright you've never
        heard of, and they all begin to discuss him.

   A. You ask who he is and what he's written.

   B. You talk around the fact that you're ignorant
        and hope for a clue.

   C. You keep your mouth shut until the subject
        changes.

▶ 4. On the job your boss gives you an assignment you
        feel is all wrong.

   A. You question the assignment and tell him
        your reasons.

   B. You obey the assignment, but look for some
        way of covering yourself when it hits the fan.

    C.   You do as he tells you, but feel miserable all day. What if it all blows up and you're responsible?

▶ 5. At the checkout counter of your local supermarket there's a rude clerk who badmouths the person ahead of you. When your turn comes, you realize she has overcharged you ten cents on one item.

    A.   You call her on it, and if she's unpleasant demand to see the manager.

    B.   She really has a big mouth and you don't want to tangle with her, but you've been cheated so you take your sales slip to the manager and complain.

    C.   What the hell, it's only a dime, and the whole thing isn't worth the badmouthing she'll give you. Let it go.

▶ 6. You're at a large cocktail party and you realize, once you've got your drink, that you don't know a single soul.

    A.   You walk up to anyone who looks interesting and say, "Hello. I'm so-and-so," and start a conversation.

    B.   You look around for the hostess and amble over hoping she'll introduce you.

    C.   You stand around awkwardly waiting for someone to start talking to you.

▶ 7. You're in line to see a movie, and when you turn to talk to someone behind you, a stranger cuts in line ahead of you.

    A.   You tap the stranger on the shoulder and say, "Look, I was here first. If you want to cut in, try it somewhere behind me!"

B.   You don't like his looks, but you were there first. In a carrying voice you tell your friend what you think of line crashers.

C.   You're near enough to the front to get a good seat. Why risk an argument?

▶ 8.   You've met this wonderful person. The sexual chemistry is just right, and you're sure you're both in love. It's come to talk of marriage, but the problem is, your religions are different.

A.   You're in love and somehow it will work out. Plenty of interfaith marriages do.

B.   Why risk marriage when an affair will do? We can live together awhile.

C.   We ought to break it off as painlessly as possible.

▶ 9.   You're at a social gathering with your new lover, and you suddenly realize from the conversation that the guests all have very different political views from yours.

A.   You speak up and defend your views.

B.   You discuss the subject without making your own views definite.

C.   You keep quiet and hope they change the subject.

▶10.   You are out with friends and your newly met lover makes a remark that you find extremely embarrassing.

A.   You challenge him/her openly.

B.   You speak to him/her about it later.

C.   You forget it. Why take a chance on spoiling a new relationship?

▶SCORING

You can give yourself 10 points for all the A answers you gave—providing they were honestly given—8 points for each B answer, and 6 for each C. If your total score ranges from 80 to 100, you are quite a gambler and you have a high risk factor. If you score between 70 and 80, you'll take a sensible amount of risk if necessary, and you have a moderate risk factor. A score below 70 indicates trouble in risk taking, a low risk factor.

BUILDING CHARLIE UP

So you tested yourself and you found yourself on the short end of the stick with a score below 70. You're one of the many people who fear failure and the humiliation of being turned down. Most of us have some degree of these fears. Nobody likes to be rejected, but there are people, like Mark, who scored a straight 100 on this risk test.

Mark is still a bachelor, but out of choice. In his early thirties, he is an executive in a small computer firm. "But I'm changing jobs next week," he confided. "It's a new outfit, just getting started. In fact, I'm taking a slight cut in salary."

"But the outfit you're with is very successful," we said, somewhat surprised. "Why take a chance on something new and unproven?"

"Because the potential is greater. I've gone as far as I can with this company, simply because it's small. The new outfit is starting big. Sure, it may go under, but it has a very good chance of surviving. I like to go for the long shots. I may fail, but if I were afraid of failing I'd be afraid of trying, and I'd never get anyplace. You know, that's true in business or on a personal level. I meet a woman I like, I take a chance. I date her, become intimate. If it doesn't work out I'm no worse off. One of these days I'll meet Miss Right and settle down. But hell, if I don't keep trying how will I ever find her?''

Charlie, who scored a measly 70 on the risk-factor test, said, ''That's all well and good for Mark. He's a natural dynamo, a guy who really enjoys a challenge. Me, I'm a regular Caspar Milquetoast. I see a woman at a party and I think she's great, and I begin trying to get up enough nerve to talk to her, fighting down all the *What if she says get lost? What if she just turns away? What if she has a guy? What if—what if*—and before I can get to the point of walking up to her, someone else has done it, and that makes it even worse.

''What can I do to give myself true confidence, to get up enough nerve to take a risk?''

What Charlie can do, what anyone like that can do, is to start small. Take a minor, unimportant risk and see if you survive. We learn how to take risks when we are still children. If the first risk succeeds, we're better able to take the next one—and a bigger one after that.

But even if the first few don't succeed, the child is driven by a developmental urge to keep trying, to learn how to eat with a spoon, to drink from a cup, to walk, to talk, to become increasingly independent, and think more and more of himself. If the child is raised properly, each success will be encouraged and he'll have the strength to go on in spite of any failures.

But if the early steps, the early attempts at independence, are in one way or another discouraged by overpro-

tective parents, if the failures are made much of and the
successes denigrated, the child may grow up unable to
take risks, or if he can he might go through terrible
doubts before any, even minor risk.

As an adult, such a person must make up for all his
early discouragement, and the best way to start is with an
easy risk—even a distant risk. We suggested that Charlie
try bucking the bureaucracy. "Call the telephone company or your utility company or even one of your credit
cards. Complain of a minor error on your bill, and let
yourself get angry. Tell them off. It's safe because you're
not in a face-to-face situation. You don't know the person
at the other end, and it doesn't much matter if they insult
you. You're only risking the price of a call, and you can
hang up at any time."

Charlie tried it and it worked. How could it fail? But
what had he accomplished? He had taken a chance on
getting out his anger and annoyance—and he had survived.

His next step was a face-to-face confrontation with a
stranger in a setting that wasn't important. We decided
on a waiter in a restaurant. Charlie complained about a
dish that wasn't properly prepared and sent it back. "It
took a hell of a lot of nerve, but I was amazed when they
brought me something else at once and apologized.
Maybe it was just the waiter's job to do that, but it made
me feel better, more confident."

Bit by bit Charlie's confidence in risking was built up.
He took a taxicab and told the driver the route *he* wanted
to go, and he insisted on it. He tried a few other confron-
tations. Some of them worked; others didn't. There were
times when Charlie was put down and humiliated, but—
and it's a tremendous *but*—he learned that he could

survive these failures. He could experience failure as well as success, and he learned that losing is not the end of the world.

EXERCISING THE ASSERTION MUSCLES

A psychiatrist we talked to told us about a program he uses with patients who are afraid to take risks. "I teach them how to use their assertion muscles, to take the risks that many people take as a matter of course. Actually, I have them go through a series of exercises."

"What are the exercises?" we asked.

"First there are some warm-up stretches, which may vary according to the patient's problem. With one young man who had a terror of being rejected by women, I said, 'At the next party you go to, walk up to two women you don't know and start talking to them.' That's a big step."

Another warm-up is to go into a cafeteria and sit down at a table with a strange woman. Start talking to her. "It's something you would think anyone could do," he explained. "Sharing a table in a cafeteria is very normal, but it was a tremendous job for my patient."

For a woman who had trouble asking for things, a warm-up was to go into a coffee shop, sit down at the counter, and ask for a glass of water without buying anything. It's a rough experience, but a strengthening one.

Once the warm-ups are past you are ready for some graduated risks. There are three plateaus in risking, and when you've attained one you must wait and practice for a while before going on to the next. You must become comfortable at each plateau. Here are four situations that will bring you to the first plateau.

1. Tell someone off—someone you work with, your lover or mate, a friend, or a brother or sister. It shouldn't be someone with power over you, but someone who is an equal.

2. Make your husband, wife, or lover do something *you* want, something he or she is not eager to do: go to a particular place for a vacation, a certain restaurant, a movie, a show—one *you* want to see.

3. At work, ask for the day off. Don't give a reason. Simply say it's for personal matters.

4. If you are unmarried, accept a blind date.

In all of these exercises failure is as important as success, because it teaches you that you'll still be able to show your face when people say no. If you succeed in the risk it proves that you may very well get what you ask for.

Once you've learned to function comfortably on the first plateau you will find that your inner self is stronger and it's time to try for the second plateau.

1. If you're single, risk going to a singles bar and talking to at least five strangers. If one appeals to you, suggest a date. If singles bars turn you off, try picking someone up at a museum or in a movie line.

2. Ask your boss for a raise. Tell him you realize this will mean more responsibility and you're prepared for it.

3. Tell your lover just what you like sexually.

Once you've reached the second plateau and survived, search for other risks that are just as threatening. The nature of the risks you select should tell you something of your strength at this point. When you've taken them and still feel capable of going on, you're ready for the highest plateau. Pass this level comfortably and your inner self is strong enough to let you deal with the world with ease.

But you must be aware that these risks should not be taken lightly. You must be ready to accept their dangers as well as their rewards, and at this level the dangers may be very real. The most important point to remember is that you cannot succeed in anything without taking a risk, whether it is love, business, or life itself. The second point is that you can survive failure.

Erica, a talented artist and a very beautiful woman, saw us a few days before her third marriage. "I know I'm taking a risk," she confided, "even though there's a strong sexual chemistry between us. He's a great guy, but I've been married twice, and both were disasters."

"But you're ready to risk a third."

She shrugged. "Sure, and I'll tell you why. If this doesn't work out, I'll probably risk a fourth. The thing is, each time my marriage failed I was devastated. I thought I couldn't go on, couldn't make it alone. But I did. I survived each failure, and I've learned that if, God forbid, anything goes wrong this time I'll survive that too."

And we knew she would. Erica is a survivor—but then, all of us can be survivors. What we need is the strength to try, and if we fail, the strength to weather the failure and go on to another try.

There is one other warning that must be given to those learning to risk. Along with risking, there is responsibility. If you take a chance, you have to be prepared to take the consequences. Leave one lover for another and you take the chance that the second won't work out.

Taking a lover is a risk, and so is marriage. Each partner gives up a certain freedom, hoping to gain more than is lost. Changing jobs is a risk. Going out on a date is a risk. Making love is a risk. But then, as one friend put

it, "You take a risk when you go out the door and cross
the street. Do you know the number of fatal auto acci-
dents that happen each year?"

But without risks life would be intolerable. We would
never move ahead. Erica's willingness to take a risk on
another love, another marriage, is less an act of daring
than an act of living. It all boils down to the fact that
risking is an essential part of life—and as for sexual
chemistry, it simply cannot proceed without risks.

8
Labeling

THE WORKAHOLIC

Risking can increase our self-esteem, can strengthen our inner selves, but we must have some understanding of just what this mysterious and often-used word "self" is before we can do much about it. There is, of course, our physical self, and a few minutes in front of a full-length mirror can tell us a lot about that: how tall or short we are, how thin or fat, how attractive or unattractive, our hair color, our eye color, and all the other elements that make each of us unique.

But there is that other self, the inner self, the name we give to the unifying force that ties together all the different aspects of our personality. One important part of that self is what we think we are, and the happy truth is that we aren't always aware of what we think. All of us have a "core" personality that remains relatively stable, but the "self" seems to float free of that personality and shift and change as circumstances differ.

This is pretty good news for all of us who aren't overly thrilled with the "self" we have. It means that "self" can be changed. If we have a problem with sexual chemistry, and that problem is related to self-esteem, it can be solved.

Craig is a prime example of someone with just such a problem. We talked to him in his small town in the Midwest, where he works in the service department of a car dealership.

Craig is that delight of employers, a workaholic. He's one of the best auto mechanics in town, and loves his job. He comes in before the shop opens and stays long after it closes, and on weekends he's completely happy working on the two half-dismantled cars in his back yard.

"The trouble is," Craig admitted, "the only real pleasure I get out of life is my work."

"What about your social life? What about women?"

Craig snorted. "What social life? You gotta be kidding. As for women, forget it. They turn off just looking at me."

We found that hard to believe. At twenty-three, Craig is tall, good-looking, and smart. His problem, he explained, was that he didn't have social graces. "Like I go to a party and I get a drink and sit in a corner watching the other guys dance and kid around with the girls. It looks so easy for them, but I just don't know how to do it myself. When I talk to a girl, my palms get all sweaty. I stutter and stammer, and I know that in a couple of minutes she'll find some excuse to take off."

In defense, Craig went to fewer and fewer parties, and threw himself into his work. He got his satisfaction out of being the best mechanic in town—enough, he assured himself, to skip the social events he was invited to. The more he was praised at his job, and the more people who insisted that Craig and no one else handle their car, the more he buried himself in his work. "The point is"—he shrugged—"I'm a jerk with women, and I'd better get used to that. At least I'm a damned good mechanic!"

What Craig had done to himself was revealed in that last statement. He had given two labels to his inner self: a *jerk* with women and a *great mechanic*. All of us, in one way or another, attach labels to our inner selves. Somewhere along the line we decide that we are either good or bad, clever or stupid, handy or clumsy, careful or careless—the list could go on endlessly.

When the label we hang on our self is good, we're ahead of the game. It affects us in a positive manner. Let a woman be firmly convinced that she's a sexpot and she'll act like one and usually be perceived as one. Let a man label himself brave and he'll be brave in most circumstances. The labels convince us of what we are—so much so that all Craig needed to act like a jerk with women was the label *jerk*. Craig carried a few other labels around with him, and one was *workaholic*. In fact, he took some pride in being one. In a way it made up for his awkwardness with women—at least in his own mind.

Before we can get rid of our labels, at least the bad ones, we have to discover them, explore them, and learn the simple facts about them. Are they true or not? To get at this with Craig, we asked him how he had felt at the last party he went to. He answered, "Awful! I was uncomfortable. It was kind of like a discothèque and there were too many people, all milling around. It was a small place, and all that noise . . . I just wanted to get out."

A friend of his who had been at that party described it

differently. "What a great scene! They had strobe lights and we were all close, real close, and they had fantastic rock music, and there was all that fabulous touching and contact. I felt terrific, and my feelings spilled out. I had a sensational time!"

Listening to both, you'd never believe it was the same party. Which of the two was right, Craig or his friend? In a way, both were. The difference lay in each one's perception of the party. Our perception of what happens to us and our reaction are not only caused by the label we put on our inner selves, they also cause the label or strengthen it.

CHANGING THE LABELS

Barbara was an old hand at hanging labels on herself. Sue, her friend, happily married now, was very disturbed at Barbara's single state. "Fred wants to fix you up with one of the men in his office. What do you say?"

Barbara agreed reluctantly. "It's not that I don't want to meet men," she told Sue. "I'd love to. It's just that they don't seem interested in me. Somehow I turn men off. I'm just not attractive, I guess."

"Nonsense," Sue said firmly. "You're a very pretty girl, and Gil will be crazy about you."

Gil was interested, but he didn't get much of a chance to talk to Barbara or get to know her. In spite of all Sue's urging, Barbara kept retreating to the kitchen to "help out." During the meal she spent most of the time talking to Sue, "girl talk," and afterward she insisted on helping with the dishes.

Predictably, the evening was a disaster. Barbara had

labeled herself a girl men weren't interested in, and she
set about making the label true. When Gil didn't get in
touch with her again, she was confirmed in what she
expected of herself. She knew she was a dud, and she
turned out to be right. Sexual chemistry never had a
chance.

If we expect to amount to something in the game
between men and women, if we hope to ignite sexual
chemistry, we have to have the right material for the fire,
and that includes a positive view of our self and a good
portion of self-esteem—and that's not possible with negative labeling.

Reexamine the labels you give yourself. Do you consider yourself inept, a lousy lover, unable to excite someone else? Really examine your thoughts about your
abilities and try facing yourself honestly. If you have any
of these negative labels, when did you first begin to use
them? Was it that first date when things didn't work out?
The first time you tried to make love and everything fell
apart?

Barbara, urged by Sue, went to a therapist to get some
help in understanding her problem. Her negative labeling about men had started, she discovered, when she
dated Tom, a boy in junior high school. It was her first
date, and Tom took her to a movie and then to a hamburger joint. He was critical of her dress, told her she
didn't understand the movie, and at the hamburger place
spent most of the time flirting with a couple of girls in
another booth. It was a devastating experience for Barbara, and remembering it made her realize that her
negative feelings about herself started then.

When she told Sue what she had discovered, Sue
nodded knowingly. "Tom! For God's sake—I went out

with him once, and the guy was a total creep. No wonder you had a lousy time. I never talked to him again."

Sue had been able to shrug off that date and realize that the fault was Tom's. Barbara had turned it around and decided that the fault was hers. The labeling started because of Barbara's own low self-esteem.

Can you change the labeling you give yourself? Can someone who's always considered himself a loser start thinking he has a winner's potential? It can be done. Therapy helps, as it helped Barbara, but most of us aren't prepared to go into therapy to increase our chances of sexual chemistry, and truthfully, most of us who give ourselves negative labels don't need therapy. Sometimes a little common sense will do wonders. Friends or relatives who genuinely like us can often be objective about us and open our eyes to what we're doing. They can point out the real situation and how different it is from what we perceive.

We were able to help Craig get over his negative labeling by simply pointing out the truth. "I'm great at my job," he told us a number of times, "but I just can't seem to talk to women."

We wondered about that. We had seen him talking to the women who brought their cars in, and we'd seen him joking around with the secretary and cashier at the showroom, free and easy. "What about those two girls?" we asked. "They're close to your age, and you don't have any trouble with them."

` "Oh, but they're different," he said quickly. "They work here. I know them, and anyway, they both have boyfriends."

"And the women who bring their cars in?"

"They're different too," he said lamely. "They're . . . well, customers."

What he was saying, in effect, was that these women were no threat. The women who worked there were spoken for and couldn't put him down. The customers depended on his goodwill. He could relax and be himself with them. But in spite of his quick protests, Craig became quite thoughtful. He began to reevaluate the labels he carried around.

Andy, one of the mechanics who worked with Craig, had a reputation for clumsiness. He dropped tools and snapped the heads off bolts—things all of them did. But Andy was labeled *clumsy*, and when he did something clumsy the label was reinforced. He'd mutter about how clumsy he was, all thumbs, and his co-workers picked it up. "Andy the klutz" became a joke in the shop.

Intrigued with the slowly dawning truth about his own labeling, and with the fact that he might not be all that stupid with women, that he could begin to change his labeling, Craig approached Andy. Flushed with his own perception, he asked, "How are you at sports, Andy?"

It turned out Andy was a fantastic basketball player, very well coordinated; he hoped to eventually get into pro basketball. "Anyone as well coordinated as that can't be such a klutz," Craig told him confidently. "What's all this clumsy shit anyway, an act?"

Andy shrugged. "What I do at work has nothing to do with what I can do on the court," he protested, but Craig's probing set him thinking, and within a week he was no longer dropping tools and had stopped the entire clumsy bit.

"Damn it," Craig told us, "if Andy can do it with his

work, I can do it with women. No more negative labeling. It's positive from here on in!''

MIND TAPES

The labels we attach to ourselves put us into broad categories: brave, clumsy, a good lover, a sexpot, a loser, a jerk. Once we fix the labels in place, we begin playing "mind tapes," internal recorded cassettes that emphasize the message on the label.

If Barbara has labeled herself a *loser at love,* she may find the courage to go to a dance, but once there she'll decide that she hasn't a chance. She'll push an imaginary button that starts her mind tape going. *I'm too unattractive for anybody to ask me to dance.* This confirms the label she has attached to herself. *I might just as well leave early.* Her label decides what she should do: leave early. This, incidentally, makes it certain that no one will ask her to dance. And as she gets her coat from the cloakroom, she thinks, *Isn't it typical of me. I come to a dance to meet people and then leave before I get a chance to. I'm really a born loser.* Leaving early has strengthened the label she has given herself—*a born loser at love.*

We all play these mind tapes in one form or another, the same message over and over. Until Barbara got some therapeutic help she kept replaying, and strengthening, her own negative tape—and ended up even more of a loser.

But any tape cassette can be changed. You can wipe out portions or rerecord the entire thing and play back a different message. The trick to rerecording a mind tape, and thereby changing a negative label, is to catch yourself when you are feeling particularly down and realize what you've said to yourself at just that moment. A good way of doing this is to force the issue. Make yourself do something you hate to do, something your intelligence tells you is good for you. Ask someone for a date. Talk to an attractive stranger on a bus. Try to pick someone up in a museum, or in a singles bar. Extend yourself with a positive attitude.

It doesn't matter what kind of reaction you get. What matters is what you tell yourself. Immediately afterward write down exactly what went through your mind before you went up to the stranger, during your talk, and afterward. Now you have your mind tapes down on paper. How do they run? If you said something like "I like the looks of that person. Maybe I can get a date," then you're playing a positive mind tape, and you're in good shape.

If it went differently—"Oh God, I'll be told to get lost!" or "He/she'll think I'm desperate because I made the first move"—then you know you're playing a negative mind tape.

The next step is to contradict each mind tape with a contrary view. Change "Oh God, I'll be told to get lost!" to "Won't it be great if he/she says yes?" Change "Of course she turned me down. I'm a jerk!" to "So she said no. That's her loss. Let's see who else looks interesting."

Once you've produced this contrary view in writing, practice using it the next time you approach someone at a bar, a museum, or a party. Tell yourself, first, that you have a good chance, and second, that it doesn't matter if you're turned down. You'll go on to try someone else.

The ultimate in optimistic, positive mind tapes belonged to the young man who walked down an avenue and asked every woman he passed to go to bed with him. A friend, seeing him do this, was astounded. "Do you ask every woman you meet to go to bed with you?" the friend asked.

"Every woman," the young man said firmly.

"God! You must get your face slapped a hell of a lot."

Grinning wickedly, he answered, "Yes, but I also go to bed with a hell of a lot of women!"

The moral behind the joke is that enough attempts will result in success, though it's hoped the attempts will be a lot subtler than this. The point is, you must have enough self-esteem to keep trying. One way to that strong self-esteem is through playing the right kind of mind tapes. You're bound to have some success if you keep trying, and even one success will stroke your battered self-esteem. Each continuing success will stroke it a little more and make the positive mind tapes easier to play. Eventually that negative label can be changed to a positive one. *I'm not so bad as a lover* instead of *I'm a loser in love.*

GETTING ALL THE FACTS

Sometimes the label you originally gave yourself can be all wrong because you didn't have all the facts at your disposal. Sandy was an attractive woman who wasn't very sure of herself. She tended to see anything bad that happened to her as a result of her own inadequacies.

"Maybe I'm just too critical of myself," she told us. "Whenever something goes wrong I try to think of what I've done to spoil it. It was like that with Jack. I met him at Angelo's. That's a glorified pizza-disco joint that we all hang out at. Their pizza is fantastic, and they have a little dance floor and great taped hard rock. Jack turned me on, and I could sense a real sexual chemistry going between us.

"We danced together for most of the evening, and then he asked me if I'd like to ride back to town on his motorcycle. I said, 'Great!' and I told the girls I'd come with to go on alone, and we took off with me on the seat behind him holding his waist for dear life. What a ride! We ended up at Jack's apartment and made love that night.

"I don't do that on a first date, but there was that chemistry going between us. Well, chemistry or not, I didn't hear from Jack after that. It serves you right, I told myself. You were too eager, too hot to trot. He probably has no respect for you now and you can just forget about him.

"Well, I tried, but it took a hell of a long time to get over him, and there was a lot of damage to my ego. I began to label myself the kind of girl who just can't hold a man, and sure enough, somehow or other when I met a guy I liked I'd manage to louse up the affair after one or two dates.

"Then, two years later, I ran into Jack coming out of a movie downtown. I was alone and so was he, and he seemed genuinely delighted to see me. 'Come and have some coffee and let's talk. You look great—hey, are you still single?'

"I told him I was, and he said, 'Fantastic. I want to see you.'

" 'You had a chance to do that two years ago,' I told him bitterly. 'How come you never called?'

"He looked uncomfortable. 'I couldn't,' he said honestly. 'You see, I was getting married in a few weeks.

What you and I had that night was sensational, but how could I tell you I was engaged? And why call? I knew what I felt for you was too strong. It would have ruined my marriage, so I tore up your number.'

"I was stunned. Was this really the truth? 'And now?' I asked.

" 'I'm divorced. The marriage was a mistake, and I should have known that the night we got together.' He took my hand then and said, very seriously, 'Let's try again, please!'

"Well, we did, and the chemistry is still there, and I think it's for keeps!"

The point of Sandy's story was that without knowing all the facts behind her brief fling with Jack, she had attached a negative and self-defeating label to herself. Once she decided that she couldn't hold a man, she usually arranged things, without being aware of what she was up to, so that each affair petered out. Each disaster only reinforced her own idea about her inability to be a winner at love.

Had she had the strength, at the very beginning, to shrug off Jack's silence as something that was no fault of hers, she would have been better off.

THE SPICE OF DANGER

"We met cute," Bette told us, "just like in one of those old Doris Day movies. Tim and I were trapped in an elevator for two hours. It was a big office building, and I was hurrying to get to a business lunch, and Tim, who works in the same building, was on his lunch break. I got on at the twentieth floor, and Tim at the eighteenth. We were the only two in the elevator, but I didn't even notice him when the door closed. You know how it is with elevators. You look everywhere except at the other passengers.

"I was watching the lighted numbers that marked the floors—17, 16, 15—and then we stopped and the doors didn't open. For a second or two we just stood there, and then I realized that we were stuck and panic set in. I'm not all that good in emergencies. But Tim was fantastic. He told me not to worry, and pointed out that there had never been a serious elevator accident in the city. 'We'll just be stuck a little while till they get it going,' he assured me, and he opened the cabinet where they keep the emergency phone and managed to reach someone in maintenance.

"Well, the 'few minutes' dragged into hours, two hours. I really had to fight to contain my panic. I was all keyed up, and Tim was gentle and considerate, joking and laughing to cheer me up. You know, ordinarily Tim isn't my type, but trapped there like that, all the barriers between us came down. When we finally got out—they opened the doors and Tim had to boost me up four feet— I was just ecstatic. We traded telephone numbers, and I knew he'd call me and I also knew I wanted him to. There was sexual chemistry in that miserable elevator. We've been an item ever since."

The sexual chemistry that sprang up between Bette and Tim had its roots in a psychological truism. Anxiety, oddly enough, can act as a catalyst for love. We explained earlier that the one thing necessary for sexual chemistry to work is emotional arousal, and it doesn't seem to matter how that arousal occurs. It can be a pretty face, a hairy chest, or a show of intelligence or wit. It can be special eye contact or the right kind of clothes. It can be visual or intellectual, a memory of another love—or even a fantasy.

But strangely enough, while the emotional arousal may be as pleasant as receiving a special gift or watching a beautiful sunset, it may instead be unpleasant. It can be as unpleasant as the two hours in a stalled elevator were to Tim and Bette. It was a shared unpleasantness, and the important part of this angle of sexual chemistry is the sharing.

One of the men we talked to told us that his favorite place for meeting women was an art museum. "Something about the pictures revs up a woman's receptivity," he told us seriously. "It makes them very prone to an approach. I don't know what it is. Maybe all those works of art get them into a sentimental mood—or maybe it's just that the pictures give us something to talk about, or maybe it's the energy emanating from the art that heightens our senses."

A young woman told us she favored bars. "Bars are noncommittal. You walk in, you walk out. They allow for options that don't exist in most meeting places. Of course, there's an element of danger there too. You take a risk with every stranger you meet, and while a sensible part of me says you're crazy to get involved with someone you don't know—remember *Mr. Goodbar*—another part loves the excitement of it, the very fact that it's a chance. I find it very easy to respond when there's that added spice of danger."

Experimental evidence for the fact that anxiety was responsible for sexual chemistry in these situations comes from a very clever experiment by two researchers from the University of British Columbia in Vancouver. Drs.

Donald Dutton and Arthur Aron tested men on two types of bridges. One was ordinary and secure. The other was a rather terrifying suspension bridge overlooking a 230-foot gorge. It swayed dangerously, and crossing it was a slow, scary process.

Men who had crossed both bridges were approached by attractive women with questionnaires to be filled in. The questions were prepared so that a "profile of sexual content" could be evaluated. A higher sexual content was found in the answers of the men who had crossed the dangerous bridge. The interviewers also gave the men their phone numbers "in case they wanted any further details." A far greater number of men who had crossed the dangerous bridge tried to contact the interviewers and ask for a date.

Fear, the researchers concluded, helps to create an atmosphere for sexual chemistry. This may be one reason those risky affairs outside of marriage may be so attractive. The element of danger is always present.

THE BABBLING BLOCK

While anxiety may excite sexual chemistry, there are times when it can be a block to it. The very nervousness that leads to an increase of the tension between two people, that prepares the field for receptivity, can also lead to a blocking of emotion—and a blocking of sexual chemistry.

Judy has this problem. "The thing is," she told us, "I always louse up just when things are going perfectly."

"Louse up how?" we asked.

"Well, take last month. I was on a ski weekend, and I

met this guy on the slopes. We were both at about the same level of competence, or incompetence, and we were trying the same runs. We started competing, you know, nothing serious but just having fun, and at one point he asked me if I was with anyone. I said no, and he said good, could we have dinner together that night?

"It seemed just perfect. You know, you go to these things hoping to meet someone and so often you're disappointed. But here it was, the first day on the slopes, and I was paired off for dinner, and with a great guy. I liked him. He had that clean, fresh look and a wiry muscular body. Then dinner—and disaster!"

"What happened?"

"I was so excited, so nervous, so anxious to make a good impression that I just kept chattering away, the original babbling brook! Talk, talk, talk about everything and anything—and really nothing at all. At first he listened, smiling, and then the smile became very fixed, and then he listened without smiling, and somewhere, before dessert, he just turned off and stopped listening at all. I could see it happening, but I couldn't do anything to stop it. The poor guy couldn't get a sentence in edgewise, and the awful thing is, I knew what was happening, and the clearer my knowledge became, the more I babbled."

"But why? What kept you going on like that when you knew it was wrong?"

"I've asked myself that. I think it was just my own anxiety, wanting so desperately to make an impression, and yet, with my words, blocking any real communication. I could see the sexual chemistry that had started out on the slopes dwindling away in the dining room. He spent the rest of the weekend avoiding me, and I tell you, he didn't have to work hard! I was too humiliated to face him again."

Too much talk can create a verbal barrier, as it did with Judy, but there are times when too much silence can do the same thing. Dick, who's an executive in a growing art agency, told us that he tried, whenever possible, to get some sort of sexual chemistry going between his clients and the people he hired. "Not that it has anything to do with sex," he explained, "but it's a way of relating to each other. There are some people you hit it off with perfectly, as if you both use the same shorthand. You have something going, a moment of recognition, of instant liking, that makes working together very easy and in the end profitable. It's a chemistry of sorts, and when I have it with an artist things work out perfectly. I can explain my concept and he or she flashes in on it at once.

"Well, a while back I had a really important client with a darned good account. I needed just the right artwork for the campaign, but more than anything I needed the sort of artist who could understand exactly what I wanted, whom I could work with. My usual artist wasn't available, but there was one guy whose work was terrific. I had seen his portfolio, and I had him up to the office to work on the account. We really could have done something, but it just didn't jell. There was absolutely no chemistry between us."

"But why?" we asked. "What was wrong?"

"I guess it was a kind of blocking. Every idea I threw out, he ignored—or rather he didn't respond, which seemed to me the same thing. Okay, you don't like an idea, you fight it, or you work around it, discuss it, change it, and maybe hammer out a new concept. This guy just sat there silently. Once or twice he'd say yes or

no, and that was all. I found myself doing all the talking
at first, and then I just backed off. There was no feedback, no sense of communication. I finally gave up and
told him flat out we couldn't work together—and he just
shrugged, picked up, and left. What a downer!''

Dick's "downer" isn't uncommon. There are people
who are so silent, so blocked in communication, that any
kind of communication with them is impossible. When
you're with them you inevitably feel yourself talking too
much, saying things you don't mean to, to fill in the gap
left by their silence As a result, you too usually fall back
on withdrawal and silence as a defense.

What causes the silence is hard to tell, but just as too
much talking may be caused by anxiety, too much silence
can be due to the same thing. An overanxious person
may react by withdrawing and falling into silence for fear
of saying the wrong thing. It's possible that Dick's artist
was just too anxious about getting the job.

THE ODD COUPLE

As bad as these two blocks are, too much talk and too
little talk, it gets even worse when someone who talks too
much—not out of anxiety, but out of habit or a certain
cultural background—meets someone whose background
dictates quietness. Paul and Kerry were like that. They
came from very different backgrounds. In Kerry's family,
everyone tended to be quiet. When they spoke, it was
only because it was necessary. By contrast, Paul's family
felt that sheer noise was communication. His family was
a riotous, boisterous group where everyone shouted and
constantly interrupted each other.

"Their normal noise level is a college cheer," Kerry

said. "When Paul took me to meet them we were at a pretty serious stage. I liked Paul, and I liked his no-nonsense approach to things, his certainty about what he believed in, and his ebullient enthusiasm. It was so different from my own family. But once we got into his parents' home I saw a different Paul. His certainty seemed stubbornness, his ebullience loudness, in bad taste according to the way I'd been brought up. I kept comparing his family to mine. When we left I said, 'Thank heavens! Now we can have a little peace and quiet.'

"It was the wrong thing to say. Paul was defensive as he asked me, 'So what's been eating you all evening? You haven't said a word.'

" 'I couldn't get a word in edgewise,' I snapped at him. "All that shouting!"

" 'Shouting? At least we don't sit around like scared rabbits without opening our mouths,' he snapped angrily.

" 'So that's how you see me!' and we were off on our first big full-fledged fight. I tell you, I was amazed at my own ability to yell. I was furious. But then, my family may yell when we're angry, but Paul's yell when they're happy!"

Paul and Kerry weathered the fight. The chemistry between them was too strong to be destroyed by one fight, but when Kerry was invited to Paul's parents' again, it was a dangerous time. Their relationship was almost on the rocks. The sad thing is it could easily have been saved if both had been just a little more aware of the other's problem. Suppose Paul had gone to his brother after that first disastrous evening.

"Kerry's not like us," he might have explained. "She doesn't understand all our yelling at each other."

Perhaps Paul's brother would protest, pointing out

that their loud voices were simply their way of talking. They meant no harm by it.

Paul could explain that in Kerry's family a loud voice mean anger and hostility. "That's the problem. I don't want our relationship spoiled by my family. I love you all too much for that."

It might take some explaining, but it wouldn't have been hard for Paul's brother to side with him in keeping the family's voice level down during Kerry's visits. Kerry, once she realized the problem, could help with some understanding of what loud voices mean to Paul's family. When things between them got serious enough for Paul to visit her folks, she could enlist the aid of someone from her family as an ally. What was needed was understanding and an awareness of the problem.

Paul and Kerry did make it, but only after a number of stormy battles, and after getting someone from each family to help out. Paul's brother and Kerry's mother were enlisted to straighten out the rest of the family.

Silence was not Kerry's problem. Her difficulty was her soft voice, which was interpreted by others as shyness. "In fact," Paul confessed, "that's what attracted me to Kerry in the first place. She's so different from the girls I grew up with." But Kerry was far from shy. It was simply a case of a voice signal at odds with her personality. One of the things Kerry discovered after she and Paul became close was that she could use her softness in a manipulative way. "Whenever Paul flies off the handle I can calm him down by simply lowering my voice. It defuses his excitement."

What Kerry had learned was something we can all benefit from. Many situations can be managed by turning our voices up or down. Some arguments are won by sheer, overpowering volume, but others are settled by lowering the voice. After a while the person you are arguing with will begin to lower his, and the more rational tones lead to a more rational discussion. Often, anger and hostility can be dissipated in this way. In anxiety or panic a soft voice can comfort, sending a metamessage: *I care. I understand. I am here.*

There is also an internal feedback mechanism to voice control, just as there is to body language. The shy person with a diffident voice can bolster self-confidence by raising the volume of his voice, speaking out clearly, and finishing his sentences instead of leaving them dangling.

Nancy, whose shy voice, unlike Kerry's, was due to her lack of confidence and to her uncertainty, was able to use this feedback method very successfully. "I always had a love-hate relationship with parties," she confided. "I'd go, but if anyone talked to me I'd answer in a half mumble. It was the greatest turn-off I could use. Any interest a man had would disappear, and I could see it go, and that made things even harder."

Then a therapist Nancy was seeing worked with her to try to get her out of those verbal doldrums. "He gave me assignments. He'd say, next week on your way home, ask the bus driver for directions, or stop a man in the street and ask for the time. Force yourself to speak loudly and clearly. If he says, 'What?' you have to approach someone else. Go into a store and ask a clerk the price of a dress. Ask a friend to lend you a book."

In every case, Nancy explained, she had to make herself understood on the first try. "It made me very self-conscious about how I spoke, but in a good sense. I began to enunciate each word, and as I kept up the little assignments, my confidence grew. It became easier and easier to make someone understand me the first time."

And when she tried it out at a party? "It worked, to

my everlasting surprise. There was none of that business of his eyes drifting away to see who else was in the room. I'm a different person now, and each time I speak up my confidence increases. Now for the sexual-chemistry part!''

SILENCE AND ICE

While loudness, boisterousness, constant talking can sometimes block any effective exchange, it can also, in other circumstances, spell out friendliness and love, as it did in Paul's family. This was the case with another woman we spoke to, a Protestant from Maine who married into a New York Italian-American family. ''I've come to understand that all the noise is a sign of warmth. I revel in it now, though at first it frightened me a little. The truth is, though, if loudness is warmth, then silence can sometimes be ice—even colder than ice. My father was a cold man. He hardly ever spoke, and there were long, uncomfortable silences at home while we all waited for a word, any word to let us know he cared.

''Sometimes we'd even try to provoke him into anger to get him to say something, but once he was angry he was worse than ever. He would just withdraw completely.''

Another man we spoke to interpreted his brother's silence as disapproval. ''When I'd talk to him about my work or my girlfriends, he'd just sit there without answering, and all I could think of was how much he disapproved of me. In the end I just stopped seeing him.''

The same man told us he had just broken off with a girlfriend for the same reason. ''She rarely ever talked.

When I first met her I saw her silence as something intriguing, something mysterious. She seemed so beautiful and remote. I wanted to solve the mystery, and I fantasized that at the core there was this wonderful, warm woman. But when I got beyond the surface there was nothing, only that aloof silence, and all at once what I had interpreted as mysterious became nothing more than selfish. She was so wrapped up in herself that she couldn't see the need to communicate with anyone else. I just gave up.''

And yet, for all its blocking quality, sometimes silence can be a strong, binding force. ''When we go up to our weekend place in the country,'' a married couple explained, ''we both feel that we're running away from the city. We've had a week of hassling and tension. We've both got high-pressure jobs, and I tell you, on the ride up neither of us speaks. There's a blessed silence in the car, a warm and comfortable silence. We understand each other and there's no need to chatter away. Our very presence is a comfort to each other.''

The silence this couple falls into is a productive silence. It allows them to unwind, to think, and, if one does speak, to listen. It is far removed from the cold, withdrawn silence of anger or dislike.

Silence at the right time, in the right place, can be a potent force in creating sexual chemistry. ''I fell in love with Carol,'' Barry told us, ''on our first date. It was just an explosion of sexual chemistry. There was something about her, I don't know what, that made me understand that she cared for me, was really interested in me, and understood me. Maybe it was just an extraordinary empathy.''

Carol said, ''Empathy, shmempathy. If the truth has to

be told, it was simply a case of creative listening."

"What's that?" we asked.

"Well, I call it creative listening, though maybe there's a technical term for it. I learned it when I was very young. Dad, whom I loved dearly, was fond of giving us kids little sermons, and we all used to turn off when we heard them, and that always annoyed him and he'd turn away in disgust.

"Well, one time when I had an unhappy experience with a boy, he gave me his 'boys are like buses' sermon—'If you miss one, there'll always be another along in a little while'—and I decided to surprise him. I listened attentively, and when he was finished I repeated the last few things he had said, but using different words.

"He was so shocked that I had really listened—my repeating his thoughts in other phrases made him realize that—shocked and delighted. It made his day, and it set me thinking. I tried it with my brothers and with my friends, and it always worked."

"Let's get it straight. Just what did you do?"

"As I said, I listened, and then, to show I had listened, I fed back the last few things he said in slightly different words. You know, most people don't listen. They wait for you to finish talking so they can launch into what they have to say. When they realize you are really and truly listening to them, it puts a different complexion on the discussion. I did it with Barry when we first met, and he flipped out. He calls it empathy, but it isn't. I like to call it creative listening."

Carol's technique works, and it can generate sexual chemistry not only on a lovers' level but also in many other fields. It can put an entirely new dimension into friendship, and it is particularly effective in business.

Politicians have gotten startling results with it. Most politicians seem incapable of answering a direct question, but creative listening at least convinces the questioner that he has been heard—whatever the response.

Analyzing just why Carol's creative listening works brings us to the conclusion that one of the most potent forces in creating sexual chemistry that lasts is involvement. There is a kind of sexual chemistry that comes very quickly—and often disappears just as fast. Boy meets girl and fireworks go off. There is a passionate fling, and the fireworks die down and that is that. Not only is there no *forever after,* there isn't even *a few days after.*

"I've had enough sexual chemistry in my day to start a chemical plant," a very handsome young man told us. "But none of it ever mattered. In the beginning, I thought it was great not ever getting involved with a woman. I had my freedom with a big F. I used to tell them, 'It's fun for you, it's fun for me,' and I'd say, 'Let's leave it at that,' and then I'd hang out somewhere else for a while to keep the old love from becoming a habit—and to meet someone else."

"And now?"

"Now I don't know. My drive seems gone. What I want, what I really want, is something more permanent—a real relationship, I guess. I used to laugh when a woman talked about a relationship, but I don't know. I think now that's where it's at—but to tell you the truth, I don't know how to get there."

He could have "gotten there" through involvement. It would establish a lasting relationship.

9
Barriers and Blocks

TURNING IT OFF

In the last chapter we discussed the barriers that too much talk or too little talk erects to preclude sexual chemistry. But there are other barriers that can either stop the chemistry from ever getting started or destroy it once it does start.

It mustn't be thought that barriers, in themselves, are bad or destructive. There are times when we want the barriers as protection. If two people who feel sexually attracted are married, but not to each other, and want to protect their marriages, each may erect defensive barriers.

Sometimes the barrier is quite subtle. Twisting a wedding ring sends out a signal of *I am spoken for. Watch out!* Mentioning the fact of a boyfriend or girlfriend sends the same signal—not as definite, because boyfriends and girlfriends can be displaced more easily than husbands and wives.

When two good friends, for one reason or another, find themselves in a situation that generates sexual chemistry, they may both want to turn it off. Meryl and Chuck were such friends. Both were married, and the two couples saw each other frequently on a social basis. Both worked in computer programming, in different companies, and one June they found themselves traveling together to a convention in a nearby city.

"At first," Meryl explained, "we were delighted. Neither of us knew anyone at the convention, and we clung together in defense, both of us checking into the convention hotel. We attended the same seminars, and compared notes, ate dinner together, and that night we went up to the big circular bar on the top tower of the hotel, the one that rotates and gives you a wonderful panorama of the city.

"We listened to some jazz, and then they began playing old dance tunes and we danced together, had a few drinks and at first talked business, and then . . . I guess the drinks loosened our inhibitions, and our talk became more personal, more intimate.

"I don't know when it was, but all at once I knew that something was going on between us. I began to realize how attractive Chuck was, how much we had in common—I could never talk to my husband about my work—and how easy, how terribly easy, it would be to fall into bed with Chuck that night.

"I think we both realized it at the same time, and I think the same kind of panic hit us both. Neither one of us wanted to risk our marriage by anything as foolish as a quick affair after a few drinks. At just about the same time, we both started talking about our families— Chuck's wife, my husband, our kids. It would have been funny if it weren't so serious, but it worked. The chemistry that had been building up between us was turned off completely."

The barrier that Meryl and Chuck put up can work not only with two close friends, but also with a friend's lover or anyone else you don't wish to get involved with—a boss where involvement might be dangerous, or with any person you feel is on the taboo list. There are times when any barrier you erect may be extremely helpful, but of course there are other times, situations where you want the sexual chemistry to continue, when the barriers may defeat your purpose.

THE BUSY PLOY

A classic barrier that someone may use without being aware of the fact is the "busy ploy." According to Sally, the busy ploy ruined any chance at sexual chemistry between herself and her boyfriend.

"He's a compulsive *doer*," she complained. "Most of the time he acts as if he had a rocket up his ass. He's never satisfied with a quiet evening or a quiet day. We always have to be doing something on our dates, going somewhere, driving out to the beach on Sunday—and never mind lying in the sun, it's swimming and volleyball on the sand and a quick game of touch football with a gang of friends he'll manage to pick up. In the winter it's skiing or indoor tennis. At night it's dancing or some fast-paced show at a nightclub. He can't sit still long enough for the theater or even a movie. He's constantly on the go.

"Last year we had a two-week vacation together, and I

thought finally we'd slow down long enough for some real chemistry to take place, but no—it had to be the Club Med, with a program that took care of every minute of the day!

"I couldn't take it, and a few months ago I told him that it was all off, and do you know what? He couldn't understand why. 'We have so much fun together,' he kept saying. 'We're always doing things.' Believe me, the next guy I tangle with is going to be real mellow. If we do nothing at all it'll make me happy, as long as we have time enough to know each other!"

Sally's complaint was justified. With all the motion and activity going on, it was impossible for the two of them to get together in a serious sense. The need to fill every hour of the day with some kind of "doing" can act as a very effective barrier to the development of real sexual chemistry.

Even in a marriage this hyperactivity can interfere with growing closeness and understanding. Let one partner be consumed by a hobby to the exclusion of everything else and it becomes an eroding factor in the relationship. "My husband," one housewife said unhappily, "is a gifted model builder. He used to be a contractor, but he's retired now, and I had hoped that these retirement years would give us both a chance to get closer. He always drove himself so hard at work, worked such late hours and even brought his work home. We hardly knew each other after all his years on the job.

"Once he retired he threw himself into the building of model drag lines and steam shovels. He machines all the parts in his basement workshop, and his models are so perfect that the big heavy-equipment companies buy them from him for thousands of dollars. I suppose I should be glad that he's kept busy and that we have the extra money, but I'm not. I feel left out, neglected, just as I did during the early years of our marriage, when he worked so hard. What was it all for? Now, when we have a real chance to get to know each other, he's busier than ever, always occupied, and I sense that my feelings for him are slowly dying out."

This wife's experience was matched by a husband's complaint that his wife used housework to block off any sexual chemistry. "She's always busy. If it's not cooking, then it's cleaning or doing something for the kids. I know things have to get done, but my God, she manages to fill every working minute with some activity, and she leaves absolutely no time for us, for me and her."

Of course, the opposite side of the activity coin can also be an effective barrier. If a mate or lover is lethargic, burying his nose in a book, content to spend the night in front of the TV, it can be just as frustrating to the other partner. Too little activity is just as bad as too much, and both raise effective barriers to sexual chemistry.

SMART AND DUMB

Among the more effective barriers that eventually destroy sexual chemistry is the barrier of the mind, the intellectual barrier. Someone who is well educated, but not psychologically knowledgeable enough to size up a situation and a partner, may use an overeducated and pretentious vocabulary in an attempt to make an impression. The impression usually made is one of bewilderment.

"I liked Richard the first time we met," a young lady

told us. "He's attractive and has a nice build. I'm very athletic myself, and I look for that in a man. Then, when I found out he was majoring in modern lit at college, I was delighted. It's my field too. The trouble was, after ten minutes he turned me off completely. It was as if he had spent the day browsing through the dictionary and was determined to use every big word he came across. I mean, for Christ's sake, who uses *tendentiousness, panegyrically,* and *homoiousian* in the same sentence? Tacky! I just turned off, and that was that."

But as silly as Richard's overblown vocabulary sounded to this young lady, the opposite situation can be just as bad. Another woman we spoke to told us about a blind date she had with a professional athlete. "I almost licked my lips when we were introduced. He was one delicious hunk of a man, blond hair and those bright blue eyes, and those shoulders!

"But it took only half an hour before what I felt in those first few minutes was dead. There was absolutely nothing we could talk about. He didn't read. He knew nothing about politics, and cared less. He didn't like music, the dance, or the theater. Oh, he could talk sports, but that was it. Whatever chemistry was in the air blew right away. Now I know what men mean when they talk about dumb blonds!"

The sad thing about this encounter, we learned later, was that this athlete was not quite the boob he made himself out to be. Somewhere along the line he had latched on to the idea that women liked the strong, silent type of man, that being too smart killed any sort of sexual chemistry, and that there was something adorable about being lowbrow.

Putting on a "dumb" act of any kind is as much a

barrier to sexual chemistry as putting on an "intellectual" act. "I didn't go to college so I can't understand that statement," even said in sarcasm, is too often only a decision not to try to get to the bottom of things.

The list of barriers to sexual chemistry increases as you start to think about them. There are the "space cadets" who seem to be so out of touch with reality that they not only march to a different drummer but seem to live in an alternate universe. Johnny is like that. He forgets appointments, never gets anywhere on time, can't hold on to a job because it never seems that meaningful, and sometimes even forgets to change his clothes. "There's too much on my mind," though what the too much is is never clear.

His latest girlfriend, Martha, put up with it for a month, and then she gave up. "I really thought there was something going between us, but I'm slowly coming to realize that I'm just not that important to Johnny, not if he can forget dates we make, drift off somewhere in the middle of a conversation, or spend the entire evening in his own little world. I've had it!"

Johnny was bewildered when Martha left. He couldn't understand what had happened or realize that the absent-minded attitude he cultivated was a block to any true conversation. In a reaction to Johnny, Martha took up with a very cool, very hip character. He was definitely "with it." But this didn't last long either. "The trouble is," Martha admitted sadly, "he was so hip, so cool, that I could never get through that savvy exterior of his to discover whether there was any real feeling underneath it."

The "with it" attitude this man assumed was just as much a barrier to sexual chemistry as Johnny's "space

cadet'' act. The flaky-cool types of barriers are destructive to any real relationship, and just as destructive is the
"sexpot" barrier.

The local "sexpot" who wears far too much makeup,
bleaches her hair to a dazzling shine, and dresses in
clothes a little too tight and a lot too revealing, is putting
up as much of a facade as the town "Romeo" who keeps
count of all his "scores" and lets it get out that he's the
biggest stud at the local bar.

Neither the sexpot nor the stud is a class act, and both
are guaranteed to turn off any real sexual chemistry as
much as the facade worn by the neighborhood Miss or
Mister Proper, who is so stiff and unyielding that any
deep relationship is made impossible.

VULNERABILITY

What all of this boils down to is that barriers, no
matter what they consist of, keep us from knowing each
other, from understanding each other, and from sharing
our intimate feelings. For sexual chemistry to take place
between a man and woman—and to endure—there must
be a certain degree of opening up to each other, a certain
amount of exposure and of understanding each other's
weaknesses.

"I fell in love with Ted the night he confessed to me
that he was a coward" was Tammy's rather shocking
statement. "We had been going together for two weeks,
and we had a lot in common, but I wasn't sure of what I
really felt for him. I'm not a prude, but I'm not one to
hop into bed at the drop of a hat, either. I want to know
something about a man before I fall in love with him, and

while I liked Ted tremendously, I didn't feel that I really knew him. He was a very funny guy, and he had me helpless with laughter after ten minutes. He was great to be with, constantly entertaining, but I began to realize that his constant joking and wisecracks were just a way of keeping something back, of hiding a very private part of himself.

"Then one evening we began talking about the years before we met, and suddenly he became very serious, and all his joking and one-liners fell away and he said, 'It's funny how you forget so much about the past, and then something that happened to you years ago sticks in your mind.' When he was a kid, he told me, he and his best friend were out playing when a gang of tough kids surrounded them and demanded money.

" 'I was scared, and I started digging in my pockets for change,' Ted said, 'and then I saw an open space between two of the guys, and I charged through and kept running. I was so scared that all I could think of was getting away. My friend didn't, and they beat him up. I should have stayed and helped him, but I didn't. I was too much of a coward. Later, he wanted to still be friends, but I couldn't face him after that.' He hesitated. 'In some ways I've never been able to face myself.'

"He looked at me wryly. 'Now you know the worst about me, a real coward!' At that moment I felt such an overwhelming love for this grown man standing there looking so sad and dejected that I had to put my arms around him. 'You're no coward at all,' I told him. 'It took a lot of guts to tell me that!'

"That night, for the first time, I felt that he had torn down all the barriers his constant joking had put up, and I finally saw the real man. That moment of exposure, of his confiding his secret shame to me—that was the moment that sexual chemistry worked, the moment I fell in love with him.''

Two of the most important factors in a close relationship that encourages sexual chemistry are openness and acceptance. Ted opened himself to Tammy by exposing the shame of his cowardice. He made himself vulnerable to her rejection or scorn, and by her acceptance of him she strengthened the intimacy between them.

When you are truly intimate with another person, you can open yourself, as Ted did, without fear of reprisal.

THE SINS OF THE FATHER

In addition to the many barriers we can set up to block sexual chemistry, there are the problems we run into that block the chemistry, that take the magic out of it. Time and again in our interviews we ran into people who said they had experienced that wonderful attraction, that magical chemistry, and then, in bed, all the magic disappeared and the chemistry was neutralized into nothing.

In an attempt to gain more understanding of the problems that can undermine sexual chemistry, and of just how sexual chemistry works, we asked Dr. Avodah Offit, the sex therapist, what she believed made sexual chemistry work.

"I think you must first understand that sexual chemistry works on either the excitation principle or the relaxation principle. It sounds paradoxical that two such opposite elements as excitement and relaxation should have the same end result, but that's the peculiar contradiction of the human psyche.

"As a sex therapist, when I work with impotent men and help them to feel sexual arousal, the first thing I must do is teach them to relax. If they can relax and forget about trying to perform, forget about the tension of having to perform, if they can truly forget it and concentrate only on the lovemaking, or on satisfying their partner, the erection will usually come of its own accord.

"One of the ways we cause our patients to relax is by creating a setting that's calm and peaceful, bucolic. A tense man, a man too tense to allow an erection, may find a certain type of calm, unhurried woman very relaxing—and very sexual. With someone like that he's on his way to a solution of his problem.

"Conversely, the opposite, a very relaxed man may find no stimulation at all in a relaxed woman. To him, a tense, histrionic woman will be very exciting. She can arouse a little fear in him and bring him close to ejaculation. This, of course, is my own theory, a reason why sexual chemistry occurs so often in opposite personalities. It depends on whether that other person has an exciting or relaxing effect on you."

"And if someone is neither tense nor relaxed," we asked her, "how does sexual chemistry work then?"

"Oh, there are people in the middle who are neither terribly tense nor too laidback. They may find the interplay between them very pleasant. Sometimes one may be exciting, sometimes relaxing. They work together in a cooperative way to excite and stimulate each other."

"Your theory, then, is based on the fact that opposites attract, that sexual chemistry is at its strongest when both people have opposing personalities."

"In many cases," Dr. Offit agreed. "Of course there

are exceptions—so many exceptions that I'm not even sure my theory is the rule. But it works often enough to have some validity."

One of the exceptions to Dr. Offit's theory was explained to us by a clinical psychologist. "A patient of mine," she told us, "talked of a very fascinating incident—at least fascinating to me in terms of psychology, and perhaps useful to you in terms of sexual chemistry.

"She was at a party recently, and she was introduced to a scholar in her own field, Russian culture. He was working on a book, and sounding off at length about his work. He was an ordinary-looking man, but very supercilious, with an arrogant air of knowing it all, snide and contemptuous in his delivery, tearing down everything anyone said, but brilliant in the way he did it. I listened to her description of him, and I thought, there's a man I could really detest."

"How did she feel?" we asked.

"Now that's the fascinating part. She said that as he talked, she felt a very strong attraction, a sense of sexual chemistry between them. She wanted, almost desperately, to please him, to make him respect her, and she was able to give him two new references for his book. He was pleased, and she was delighted by his approval."

"But did she actually like his contemptuous attitude?"

"Like it? She ate it up! She told me that she found it very manly, very sexual. I had difficulty believing that, but in my practice I've run across every kind of attraction.

"I began to question her and to probe a bit, to ask her about her background, her parents, and suddenly her eyes opened and she said, 'Of course. That's it! He had the same snide intelligence that my father had. He put me down just the way my father did—and I loved it. How mixed-up can you get?'

"It turned out that her idea of attractive men, of sexy and masculine men, were those like her father, who were slightly contemptuous of her, arrogant, and flaunting their intellectual superiority.

"Our parents serve as our early role models. Not only do we pattern ourselves after the parent of the same sex, but we look for a sexual partner who reminds us of the other parent. A woman feels sexual chemistry for a man who resembles her father, even though she may be miserable with such a man. A boy will look for someone who resembles his mother. I suppose, in a way, the sins of the parents are perpetuated in the children. Certainly in the case of the woman I told you about, the sins of her father were just those she searched for in a lover."

Of course, the other side of the coin is that we also seek partners with the good qualities of our parents. If her father is a gentle, accepting man, a woman may look for those qualities in her lover—and be disappointed when she fails to find them.

10
Keeping Sexual Chemistry Alive

LOVE IN THE AFTERNOON

"The guys at the office used to kid me about taking such long lunch breaks," Michael, an accountant in his forties, told us. "Finally, just to keep them quiet, I said I was having an affair, and since I'm married and have two kids, lunch break was the only time we had together. I told it to them seriously, and they were not only impressed, but they were embarrassed enough to stop kidding me about it. Oddly enough, I gained a lot of status in the office."

"And what about this affair? Wasn't it rash of you to tell them?"

"That's the kicker. I live twenty minutes away from the office by subway, and what I've been doing at noon is hopping the train home. My wife picks me up at the station, and we spend a half hour or so making love—our matinee, we call it—then she drops me off and it's back to work. If I ever told the guys the truth they'd razz the hell out of me. An affair with my own wife! As it is, they keep quiet about it."

"But why all that trouble just to have sex with your wife? You sleep together every night."

Mike grinned. "There are half a dozen reasons, I guess. First of all, we're too damned tired at night. I don't get home till after seven, and many nights I have to work at home, and Margie has a rough time with the kids and the house. We're both played out at night. That's what started me off on this, and besides, there's something special about it."

"But aren't you going to a lot of trouble just to— well . . ."

"Go on, say it. Just to get laid. But when I was single I'd think nothing of traveling an hour or two just to take a girl home if there was a chance of scoring. The big thing about all this is, the two of us share something. It's a secret time together that even the kids don't know about. To tell you the truth, it's changed our entire sex life, spiced it up and put all the sexual chemistry back into it."

FAST BUT FABULOUS

Another married couple told us they had revived their sexual chemistry by quickies. "It started one evening when we were getting dressed to go out," Steve, a painter, told us. "I was just finishing shaving at the sink, and Marlene had come out of the shower. The mirror was fogged up from the steam, and when I wiped it off to see my face I had a glimpse of Marlene reflected in it, bending over to dry her feet. It was late afternoon, and the sun was low with that peculiar orange light, and it seemed to glow all around her. She looked exactly like a Renoir nude, and all at once I was turned on and excited. 'I've either got to paint her this second or make love to her,' I told myself.

"I wiped off the shaving cream and, turning, ran my hand down her back. Startled, she stared at me for a moment, then began to smile. It was pretty obvious how I felt, and we started hugging and kissing right there in the bathroom. 'We have to leave in a half hour if we're to meet the Thompsons,' Marlene murmured, and I said, 'We don't need a half hour!'

"We didn't. It was the quickest, most exciting love-making we had had in years. I don't know what turned us on so, the fact that we were so rushed for time or just the idea of sneaking this bit of lovemaking in when it was so unexpected and there was such a sense of immediacy.

"We were only a few minutes late getting to meet our friends, and the two of us were really high that evening. I think it was the fact that we shared an intimate secret, something just a bit furtive. We could look at each other and grin at that private knowledge."

It was the spontaneous quality of that quickie that acted as a turn-on for Steve and Marlene. It changed what had become ordinary and a little dull into something exciting and different. "We've had an occasional quickie since then," Steve said, "and each time it seems to rev up the sexual chemistry between us."

This type of quickie that shook up the routine of their sexual lives didn't take the place of the unhurried love-making of their marriage, but when it did happen it put an erotic edge on their relationship and helped ignite a spark of sexual chemistry that made their marital sex even better.

THE IMBALANCE FACTOR

Many married couples initiate fights and arguments just to keep the sexual chemistry alive. "We seem to fight like crazy during the weekends," one couple admitted. "And sometimes we don't even remember what we're fighting about. All we know is that it perks us up, makes us alive, and somehow makes sex more intense and interesting, because the fights always end with a furious bout in bed.

"The trouble is, we don't think it's right, because although it heats us both up, it also, in some way, is subtly eroding our relationship. I keep remembering the times when we didn't need the artificial heat of an argument to kindle desire."

Another, older couple had an almost philosophical acceptance of the loss of sexual chemistry. "To me," the husband said thoughtfully, "it's the memory of sex that works. When we were young I'd be turned on by seeing my wife undress, by a glimpse of her bare breast or the way her dress fell over her buttocks. There was always a drive inside me that seemed to come to life at those moments.

"Now most of the drive is gone, but the memory of how great sex was still arouses me. I initiate sex not because I need it as much as I used to, but because I remember how terrific is used to be."

A marriage counselor we talked to agreed that too often the companionate love that passionate love turns into can be associated with boredom. "The solution," she suggested, "is to alter the pattern. If you find your lover doing something that's unusual it may make you uncomfortable, but discomfort is sometimes at the core of sexual chemistry."

"In what way?" we asked.

"Well, you're back to square one in your relationship. You're facing an unknown, wanting to conquer or be conquered. You're in a primitive state of imbalance. I believe that there is a greater potential for sexual chemistry if you can keep re-creating that state of imbalance—in a positive way."

The couple who used constant fighting intuitively understood that they needed to regain their sexual chemistry, but veered off in the wrong direction trying to achieve it. Constant fighting and bickering can erode a relationship. An occasional fight is something different, and it often clears the air and starts the chemistry working again. But fighting is not necessary.

CHANGING THE CONTEXT

In previous chapters we have seen that heightened emotions can lead to sexual chemistry. There are ways of heightening the emotions without resorting to a fight. One couple we know of tried using sadomasochistic techniques in the privacy of their home, sometimes working out private fantasies each had of bondage and pain. The trouble was that this type of solution may work for a while, or seem to work, but eventually it evokes a sense of guilt. The fantasy itself becomes the only way the couple reaches satisfaction, and there is no attempt to work out their relationship. Replacing the partner in a sexual act with a fantasy figure interferes with the intimacy between the two lovers.

The couple we spoke to felt that their sexual chemistry had been renewed, but they also felt a sense of shame at the method they had used. We found that same shame in other couples who had resorted to "swinging"—changing partners or introducing a third person into their sexual relationship in an attempt to put "life" into their marriage. In the end, most of these attempts merely raise new barriers to intimacy.

Another couple used a technique based on fantasy without the accompanying stigma of shame. They would go out separately, agreeing to meet in a bar as strangers and go through the whole routine of a pickup in front of people they didn't know. It turned both of them on and created a wonderful mood of sexuality.

Here it was the unknown at work, the sense of something different, the illusion of danger or fear that, under certain circumstances, acted like the real thing.

Another method of re-creating sexual chemistry is to change the context of the relationship. "A vacation works wonders for us," a young couple confided. Both professional people with careers, they found more and more of their free time given over to work. "I come home at seven," the husband told us, "and we're both too exhausted to even fuss with dinner. We either go out to a local coffee shop and grab a bite or make a quick meal out of whatever's in the fridge. Then we both tackle the work we've brought home, and we're usually at it till eleven o'clock. We're lucky if we catch a late news program before falling asleep."

"And the weekends aren't much better," his wife added. "We're lucky if we manage a social evening on Saturday or Sunday. I tell you, when vacation time comes we're champing at the bit—but that makes it all the more wonderful. We pick our vacation places carefully, places that are new and exciting, where the stimulus of something different, things we've never seen before, people we've never met, can act. Last year we flew to England, rented a car, and took ferries to the Outer Hebrides. It was like stepping into a different world—and a different life.

"We were like two different people who had met in a new and strange place, an exciting place, and the old sexual chemistry took over. We had two glorious weeks to renew our lives."

Another couple faced with the same problem refused to wait for vacations to revive their feelings. "We take off every other weekend, work be damned, and we get away from the house and the kids. We have a baby-sitter and we check into a lavish downtown hotel. It's expensive, but we skimp somewhere else to afford it."

"I head right for the bathroom," the wife said, "and I run a hot bubble bath with perfume and just relax. Usually Carl joins me—I always check out the hotel first to make sure they have the right kind of bathrooms. We have drinks sent up by room service and then dress and have a leisurely dinner in the hotel dining room, dance and flirt with each other and prolong bedtime until the chemistry between us is in full bloom—and one or two nights will do the trick. We get back home feeling revived and renewed."

Another couple, in the suburbs, checks into the best nearby motel and more or less repeats the same ritual. With both, the point is to overcome the inhibitions that build up in a longtime relationship. They see each other in a changed setting, and in a different role. "My wife isn't a mother anymore," a young husband told us. "When we're off like that she can drop all the paraphernalia of parenthood and become the witty, amusing girl I married." And the wife, nodding agreement, pointed out, "He isn't his usual harried self. He can put his work aside and become a lover again and concentrate on me. It's flattering, and it rekindles what we once felt, what's really still there but buried under all the cares and concerns of living."

There was one couple who had a slightly different approach to the same eventual goal. "We break the pattern of things," Nora explained. "Hal will get theater tickets on a night I least expect him to, and he won't tell me about it until he's leaving work. Then he'll call and say, 'We're going out tonight, dinner and the theater. Get yourself ready.'

"Sometimes it seems as if it's a crazy thing to do. I may even have started dinner, and I'll be tired and cross and want nothing more than an evening at home, but it's always possible to freeze what I've made, or put it away for tomorrow, and somehow going out unexpectedly takes care of any tiredness. There's a festive quality to it just because it's such a surprise—and inevitably when we get home that night the air between us is charged with electricity."

MAINTAINING THE PRIORITIES

Changing the pattern of lovemaking is a subtle thing, but sometimes vacations or dinners out or theater tickets aren't necessary. The context of a relationship can be changed enough to revive old feelings without even leaving the house. You can treat a simple evening at home in a deliberately romantic way. Wine and candlelight can turn a meal into something special. Sometimes something as simple as soft background music or unexpected flowers brought by the husband, a specially prepared dish by the wife, can help recapture the excitement and unexpected little pleasures of the early days of courtship.

There are other tricks you can borrow from early courtship, little gestures that fall by the wayside in a long relationship or a marriage, gestures that die only because so much is taken for granted. You can start thinking of your partner as a lover again, and you can tell this lover the flattering little intimacies you once shared: how pretty she looks tonight, how handsome he is. If pretty and handsome are out, then you can compliment each other on all the things you once found endearing: hair, skin, eyes, body, clothes . . . Done subtly and convincingly, it can put an entirely new and fresh element into a stale relationship.

One wife told us that the context of their marriage had been changed when her husband began to approach her at unexpected moments and start making love. "Sometimes we would just forget about dinner or our plans to go out to a movie. I always saw that unexpected lovemaking as an affirmation of the sexual chemistry between us."

But this change in pattern must be approached carefully, with the other partner's reaction in mind. This particular wife reacted eagerly. Another wife we talked to complained bitterly just because her husband approached her at inappropriate times. "Why in hell does he always feel turned on when I can't react, when I'm in the middle of cooking dinner or doing some job around the house that needs concentration? That, believe it or not, is the one time he picks to get horny—never mind all the appropriate times when we're in bed together. Then he's too tired, or he has to finish reading this document or that book, or he has to get to sleep early because tomorrow's a big day. No, the times he picks for sex are always wrong, always times when I'm not able to respond!''

And yet other women have been delighted with the spontaneity of ''inappropriate'' lovemaking. ''What's so great about Les is that he can be turned on at the craziest moments,'' one wife announced fondly. ''He'll come into the kitchen and see me up to the elbows in pots and pans, and bam, he begins feeling me up, and before I know it we're making love right there and then, me reaching out to turn off the gas while Les's nibbling at me eagerly. It's silly and it's crazy and I love it. It makes me realize that I can still get that old chemistry going, even with my hands full of flour and my hair a mess and wearing my old kitchen apron. It's very flattering, a great boost to my ego.

''One morning I decided to take things into my own hands, and I started breakfast with only my apron on. Les was in a hurry to get to the office, but when he came down and saw me like that, he forgot about everything. It was one of the best mornings we've had!''

What Les has managed to do is maintain the proper priorities, convincing his wife that she's the most important thing in his life, more important than work or food, and that he'll let either one go just to make love to her. It is one sure way to keep their sexual chemistry going.

The wife who thought her husband's lovemaking was inappropriate was turned off because to her the message in his approach was his own need, his own sexual hunger, and it seemed to her he was willing to satisfy it at her expense. Her perception of his approach as selfish and self-centered was enough to turn off any chemistry she might have felt.

LAYING THE GROUNDWORK

Another suggestion given to us by a clinical psychologist was to lay the groundwork for continuing sexual chemistry in the early days of a marriage or a relationship by telling your partner what you like and dislike in lovemaking. "One of my patients, a young woman, came to me with a bitter set of complaints. Her marriage, after five years, was falling apart. 'It's been destroyed,' she told me a bit dramatically, 'in the bedroom!'

"When I pressed her to explain, she said her husband never made love the way she wanted him to, never caressed her in the right way.

" 'But have you told him what you wanted?' I asked.

"She frowned unhappily. 'No, but if he really loved me, if he really cared, he'd know what I want. I shouldn't have to tell him.'

"It took a long time before I could convince her that there was no magic formula for lovers, no instinctive knowledge of what to do and what not to do. 'It's something you both have to learn,' I explained, 'and you have to learn it together. Each partner must tell the other what turns you on and what doesn't. It should have been done at the very beginning of your marriage. It's an unrealistic expectation to think that your lover will automatically know what you want.' "

One of the reasons that sexual chemistry often dies away in a relationship, this psychologist explained, is that "we tend to make too much of a deal over sex. We continually expect fireworks, a feverish pitch of exaltation, the ultimate in emotion. We don't make that kind of a deal over other aspects of our lives. We don't expect every meal to be a four-star gourmet experience. Why do we ask so much of sex?

"I had a patient, a thirty-year-old woman who was living with a man for the first time in her life, and on many levels it was a good relationship, but very gradually she was destroying it, undermining it."

"In what way?" we asked.

"By her expectations—and worries. She was concerned about the sexual chemistry between them, worried that they weren't having enough sex, that they were having too much sex. She was always comparing her sex life to some inner standards of her own, and those standards were always different from what she experienced. She was constantly wondering if her sex life was normal, if other people didn't have it better, and gradually that came to eat away at her relationship and destroy what sexual chemistry she did have, a chemistry that could have been very satisfying.

"She was the type of woman," the psychologist explained, "who carried these doubts and worries into all aspects of her life. She'd go out in a pants suit and see a woman in a dress and decide a dress was more glamorous, or she could just as easily go out in a dress and decide that another woman in slacks was more stylish. When you come right down to it, it was an inability to accept herself as she was—just as she was unable to accept her sex life as it was, an inability to accept reality."

Another aspect of this refusal to accept reality can come about if you do not accept your lover as he or she really is. One young woman complained to us that while her lover was "good in bed, he doesn't talk easily. I like someone who's verbal."

There were many things about her partner that she

liked, she admitted, but she had trouble accepting him as he was. She wanted him to be not only good but perfect, and as a result she made herself miserable by blowing his faults up out of proportion.

The important lesson we can learn from all of this is that very often when sexual chemistry appears to fade or diminish, we search for a solution in some aspect of the chemistry itself. We ask, what's happened to the attraction that used to be between us? Where have the magic and fire gone?

In truth, the problem usually lies in the relationship rather than in the chemistry. Resentment, a sense of loss when your lover forgets to praise you for your accomplishments or tell you how attractive you are, or even the lines of communication becoming rusted and inoperative can all be a part of the real problem.

Anne complained to us that after seven years of marriage any sexual chemistry between her and her husband was gone. "I suppose I'm silly to expect it to last. It's romantic nonsense, isn't it? But somehow I feel terribly depressed about my marriage. I feel tied down, unappreciated, really just a servant to my husband and baby— but servants at least are paid and aren't expected to be available for sex!"

On questioning, it turned out that Anne's problem was not what had gone wrong with the sexual chemistry in her marriage but what had gone wrong with the marriage itself. Her husband, she admitted, had a very tough job. "When he comes home, usually late and after the baby is in bed, I know he's had it up to here with business, and he can't turn it off. Over dinner he tells me all about his work, and after dinner he may watch an hour of TV before we go to bed—and then he wants sex!

"I feel used. He never asks me about my day, about the baby or the house. Okay, it's boring to him, but it bores me too! Maybe it would be less boring if we shared it. After all, I'm bored with his work, but I share it, don't I?"

Anne is building up so much resentment toward her husband that it is impossible for the chemistry between them to work. The chemistry may still be there, but it can't take over until they are able to talk over this problem and struggle through the basic trouble between them.

11

The Many Phases of Sexual Chemistry

THE THREE LOVES OF EVE

"I've experienced sexual chemistry three times in the past seven months," Eve told us, "and each time it was with someone totally different."

"What happened to them?"

"Well, the funny thing is, I still see them, all three of them, and the sexual chemistry is still there. Of course, none of them knows I'm dating the others. I think Chris wouldn't mind. I met Chris first, and I really liked him. We have a great time together. He's almost like a brother, but a good brother, one who understands me and cares for me. In a way, our sexual chemistry is a very deep affection. We like the same things, the same sports and the same movies—we even watch the same sitcoms on TV. I used to think if I ever became serious about anyone, it would be Chris. He's so easy to live with."

"What about the other men?" we asked.

"I met Phil a month after I started seeing Chris. We

met at a party doing a game of charades. We two were a team, and we were the winners. It's funny, we had a sort of ESP with each other. I'd guess a word before Phil had started acting it out. It was a sort of instantaneous understanding. The thing is, he asked me out and I went, and you know, with Phil, love itself is a sort of game. Once he told me that love is like a good wine. You should enjoy it, but you shouldn't overindulge! That's Phil. There's sexual chemistry between us, but there's also a lot of distance.

"Funny, I've never felt untrue to Chris when I've been with Phil, because Phil has such an air of independence. He won't allow me to become too attached; he values his own privacy too much, and right now that's fine for me. I find him attractive, and yes, we've been to bed together. Sex, to Phil, is sort of a game, a pleasant pastime, he told me once. He was quoting the Roman poet Ovid. Anyway, I have fun with Phil. It's not like it is with Chris. Chris is for sharing—Phil is for fun, and I know he plays the field, but who am I to complain. You can't be constant with a guy like Phil. He wouldn't want it."

"And your third love?" we asked.

"Oh yes, Jack. That's a whole new ball game." She paused and shook her head. "I only met Jack two weeks ago, and I don't know. It's become pretty heavy. These past weeks I've felt like a juggler trying to keep three things in the air going at once, but my three things are men, Chris, Phil, and Jack. I could manage it with three like Phil, or one Chris and two Phils, but Jack's something else altogether.

"I met Jack at a concert. We had seats together, and I realized he was looking at me instead of the stage, and finally I caught his eye and he apologized and we began talking, and then he asked me out for a drink, and the next day he called me at work. He remembered where I worked from our talk over drinks, and I went out with him because . . . well, I felt such a strong sexual chemistry between us that evening after the concert, and I know he felt it too—and I was right. It's there.''

She hesitated. ''Jack is different from Chris and Phil. There's an excitement when we're together, a kind of charged energy level, and I get the feeling that he approves of everything about me. He notices things—my hair, my clothes, my eyes. I'll bet Chris doesn't even know what color eyes I have! With Jack it's so different. He knows me so completely. He wants to see me every day, and that makes a problem, because I hate to give up Chris and Phil, but I know Jack won't tolerate another man in my life.

''He wants to be very close. Oh, we've slept together, and that's exciting too. He's good in bed, damned good, and there's none of the game-playing there is with Phil. Jack is open and honest, and he's not jealous or possessive. It's just . . . well, he's so sincere, I guess that's the word. I really think if I go on with him it's got to be just the two of us, but I'm not ready to give up Phil and Chris. In a way I love them too. There's still such chemistry between us!''

THE COLORS OF LOVE

It's unusual but not unheard of for someone like Eve to be in love with more than one person at the same time. Our culture tends to consider a situation like this immoral, but our Western morality about love is based on our Western attitude toward religion. We have accepted a concept of one God, and we also, for good or bad, accept a concept of one love. We consider it immoral to be in love with more than one person at the same time, but it can happen; it happens quite often. In our interviews we ran across this type of situation frequently enough to assume that it's a part of the normal framework of love, at least one part.

The fascinating thing about Eve's three loves, and the reason we chose to tell about them, is that they are each so different from the others, and in a way they symbolize three different types of love, perhaps the three basic types.

In a doctoral thesis on love, Dr. John Alan Lee, who teaches sociology at Scarborough College at the University of Toronto, likens love and sexual chemistry to a color wheel. He finds three primary types of love, just as there are three primary colors.

The most intense, which he likens to red in the spectrum, he calls *eros* (from the Greek word for love), and it's a love that is predominantly sexual. It is very much like the love that Jack feels for Eve. It involves an immediate and powerful sexual chemistry. There is a strong sexual element to it, and it has an all-or-nothing quality. Strangely enough, there is not a great deal of jealousy in this type of love. *Eros* lovers are not possessive as much as they are exclusive. Infidelity would end the relationship, because the relationship is based on trust. Eve realized that she had to give up her other lovers if she wished to keep Jack.

The second primary type of love Dr. Lee calls *ludus*, from a Latin term for play or sport. This type of love sees the whole thing as a game, with promiscuity allowed and with a lack of commitment. Phil practiced it to perfection. He never allowed himself to become too involved, nor would he commit himself to any one woman. In *ludus* love, sexual chemistry occurs quickly, but is rarely as strong as it is in *eros* love. Phil experienced sexual chemistry with Eve, but he wouldn't allow himself to "fall in love." He never wanted to get absorbed by his lover. He was always casual and in control of his emotions, and he expected his lover to play the same game and stay in control of herself.

Ludus is a freewheeling, easy sort of love, and in Dr. Lee's color wheel it is likened to blue, a cool color.

The third primary type of love is labeled *storge* (pronounced stor-gay), from a Greek word for natural affection. It describes an affection that is close, but more like a deep friendship than a true love. Chris, who typifies this type of lover, was a friend to Eve, and she explained that there had been no sex between them. "We are just as satisfied to hug and kiss, and while we both thought that someday we might get around to sex, we were in no hurry. It's funny," she added, "I know I have to stop seeing Phil, and I know we'll both get over it pretty quickly, but I just won't stop seeing Chris. He'll always be a good friend."

And friendship is at the bottom of this type of love. In *storge* love you are not preoccupied with your lover. You are relaxed and like to do things together, to share interests and avoid manipulating each other's feelings. It's a relaxed kind of love, and Dr. Lee likens it to yellow, a bright, clear color and the third color on the wheel—red, blue, yellow.

As with colors, there are secondary types of love in Dr. Lee's listing. The secondary colors are green, purple, and orange. One of the secondary loves is *mania* (from the Greek, meaning "to be mad"), the possessive, jealous, obsessive love, between *ludus* and *eros*; Dr. Lee gives it the color purple, but we would see it as green. The love he labels green, he puts between *ludus* and *storge*; it is *pragma* (from the Greek word for deed), a pragmatic sort of love, realistic. Where orange occurs in the wheel, between red *eros* and yellow *storge,* Dr. Lee puts *agape,* the Greek word for charity and love used by Saint Paul in his first letter to the Corinthians. This is dutiful, unselfish, and self-sacrificing—and oh so rare!

BREAKING UP

The real problem Eve faced was breaking the sexual chemistry between herself and Phil and Chris when she decided the relationship she wanted to keep alive was the one with Jack. Of the three, it suited her best.

There is no moral judgment possible about the various types of sexual chemistry—and love. The only certainty is that you can probably fit any type of sexual chemistry that can occur between men and women into some slot on Dr. Lee's color wheel. He lists three more types, which are simply combinations of the three primary types, and of course there are other combinations possible.

The intriguing thing about his research is that all types of love can be fitted onto the wheel. But we cannot say that the primarily sexual, *eros* type of love that Eve felt for Jack is better than the love-as-a-game type of *ludus* love that Phil offered or the brother-sister *storge* type she shared with Chris. It was simply her choice to pick *eros.* Another woman might have been just as happy with sharing or game-playing.

Breaking the sexual chemistry between herself and Chris was very simple for Eve. She approached him with honesty and told him how she felt about Jack, and how she felt about him. "I'll always want you as a friend," she finished, and Chris, though hurt, understood and agreed reluctantly.

Phil, however, was different. Eve knew she couldn't come out with the truth without hurting his feelings, and she liked him enough not to want to do that. "I resorted to a little game-playing myself, something Phil always delighted in," she admitted.

"I began to make demands, to talk about marriage and children, about commitment—things I knew would frighten Phil off, and they did. He could only take a relationship where he was free to break off when he pleased. I sent up some wrong signals that made him do the breaking, and I left him with the feeling of being in control. He needs that!"

Breaking up is a very serious aspect of sexual chemistry. There are times when you realize, as Eve did, that the relationship is wrong and must stop, but for one reason or another you are reluctant to be the one to stop it. Eve's solution was to be manipulative with one of her lovers and forthright with the other. The method used, as she clearly understood, must be adapted to the lover— and the type of love that has been between you.

A man we spoke to had had an intense love affair that had lasted over a year. "I met someone else just two months ago, and I knew at once she was the right girl for me. The chemistry between us was perfect, and I suddenly realized that my other affair was all wrong and I had to leave her. I decided to be completely honest, and I told her why I was leaving. God! It was the mistake of my life. She carried on as if I had betrayed her, and yet there was no commitment between us, no understanding. I simply looked on it as a love affair. She saw it as the be-all of her life! She threatened suicide, threatened to call my new friend and tell her what had been going on, she begged me to reconsider—it was awful, a real downer. I was so shook up by it that now I've backed away from this new girl and I just want to be alone for a while to sort things out.''

The love affair that this man was trying to break up was, at least on the part of his lover, one of the loves Dr. Lee classes as *manic,* a jealous, possessive, obsessive love. Honesty and truth are never good approaches in these cases. He should have searched for some way of breaking off the affair without confiding what had really happened, although there was probably no graceful way he could have done it.

The lesson he learned from it all was to be extremely careful *before* entering an affair. The *manic* type of love is, in some cases, pleasing to the ego. You seem to become your lover's entire world. But this very possessive quality can also be tremendously damaging. To be someone's world is to shoulder an enormous burden, and it's a burden that isn't easily laid aside.

There are very few ways of breaking off a love affair, so it may be better to think carefully before allowing sexual chemistry to overcome you. What kind of lover are you? What kind of lover do you want? Here is a list of six of the nine types Dr. Lee has discovered. It will help you to be able to understand which suits you best and, even more important, which you would hate to be involved in. Then, when sexual chemistry does its delightful work, shake your head a bit to clear your brain and analyze just where your lover fits into the list. It should be a case of match and mate.

eros: A basically sexual type of love. You are eager to see a lot of your partner. You are verbal, tactile, open, and sincere. You enjoy sex and intense emotions.

ludus: You like a variety of types. You do not "fall in love" but continue as you were, with no intention of including your lover in your future. You maintain your privacy, see love as a game, and refuse to be too intense. It's a casual, mutually enjoyable state.

storge: Your love is like a deep friendship. Although you want to share with your partner, you are not preoccupied with the affair. You are relaxed, with no strong emotions, and you are shy about sex.

mania: This love involves intense preoccupation with your lover. You want to see him or her constantly, cannot break off the relationship, and become possessive, jealous, obsessive, and altogether miserable—which you consider a true state of love.

pragma: You know what kind of a lover you want, and you go on with life as usual when you meet her/him. You are sensible about dates, sex, and involvement, and you avoid scenes. Oh yes— you believe no one is worth sacrificing too much for.

agape: This is a dutiful, unselfish love which you offer regardless of the difficulties involved. You give your love without any regard for personal gain—and you must probably be something of a saint for this to work!

These are the three primary types of love and the three secondary types. There are of course, combinations of these—Dr. Lee lists *ludic-eros, storgic-ludus,* and *storgic-eros*—but the six primary and secondary types are sufficient for our purpose. There are very few love affairs that cannot be described by one of the six types.

TURNING IT OFF

In breaking up an affair, or in turning off sexual chemistry before it reaches the stage of an affair, your approach must depend on the type of lover you are breaking with. There is no wrong or right approach, except what is wrong or right in a given situation, but some approaches may be hard to stomach.

Charles, who considers himself something of an expert lover, surely a *ludic* type, told us he had a surefire method for ending an affair.

"Or at least I had one until I met Rona. With other girls, when I wanted to be free, to get out of a situation that had become sticky, I used to become obnoxious. I'd be late for dates or even forget them. I'd become unreliable, sullen, and selfish. I'd even louse up sexually, and turn our lovemaking into a mess. It always worked. The girl would break off first in disgust, and I'd be free—and free without any of those guilty feelings you get when you have to tell someone it's all over.

"Then I met Rona, and the sexual chemistry between us was like a thunderclap. I tell you, I was hit but bad, and I decided that this was it, with marriage at the end of the road. The only trouble was, I was dating four other women, and I knew I'd have to do some clever juggling to get them to drop me.

"But I hadn't figured with Rona. The first time I put the moves on her she stopped me. 'Okay, Charlie, let's get things straight. Is there anyone else?' I squirmed and tried to lie, but I couldn't. Rona said, 'I don't want to put you in a spot, but before we get serious you'll have to tell anyone else you're involved with the truth. I won't be part of a harem.' And she meant it.

"That was the roughest thing I ever did, telling each of those girls it was over with because I'd fallen in love with someone else. But you know, once I'd done it I didn't feel guilty. In fact, I felt very good. There's something to honesty in a relationship. Rona taught me that."

Charles has still to learn that the honesty approach works only in cases where the lover is neither jealous nor obsessive. But Charles's other method had a dishonest touch to it that, in spite of all he said, must have had a destructive effect on his self-image.

As we said before, there is no easy way to terminate a love affair, but there are certain methods that can be used, unless the affair is of the *manic* kind—jealous, obsessive, extravagant. Then no method will really help. Nothing you can say to your lover will get you out of it with grace.

If your love affair is of the *eros* type, sexual at the core, there are bound to be hurt and hard feelings on one side or the other when you break up.

Still, if Dr. Lee is correct, that leaves at least four other basic types of love affairs that can be managed rationally and reasonably when it comes to splitting—or, as Eve did, with a bit of manipulation.

The problems in the breakup of sexual chemistry can be resolved by choosing carefully at the beginning of the affair, by not allowing inappropriate chemistry to develop whether the inappropriateness is due to the wrong kind of partner or the wrong kind of situation. But can you control sexual chemistry? Can you prevent it from developing with the wrong partner? Can you turn it off when you have to?

Celeste picked the wrong man, not only in terms of an inappropriate partner, but also because he was the *manic* type of lover, jealous and obsessive. "But worst of all," Celeste sighed, "he's my boss. I don't know what to do. I realize that it's a terrible mistake, but if I try to break it off, if I even hint at cooling it, he gets furious, and I know he'd fire me—and dammit, I really need the job."

And so Celeste stays in an uncomfortable situation, hoping that her boss will be the first to cool off. "But even that isn't going to help," she admitted despondently. "If he's the one to break it off, he'll still want to get rid of me. All I can do is get out my résumés behind his back."

Jim had the reverse of Celeste's problem. He had started an affair with his secretary. "I could feel the sexual chemistry between us the first moment we met, but I just couldn't turn it off. She's such a great kid, interested in everything I am, and fun to be around. We have sex, but it's not overwhelming. It's just good." Jim's affair was *ludic*, but just as hard to break off as Celeste's *manic* one. "I should have remembered my older brother's one good piece of advice," he said wryly. " 'Don't foul your own nest—don't dirty your own doorstep!' "

The problem facing Celeste and Jim is a tough one. True, there's almost no way of preventing sexual chemistry from taking place. When it happens, it's like a bolt out of the blue, an amalgam of forces beyond your control. There's the physiological reaction, to begin with, and nothing can really prevent that.

But as inevitable as sexual chemistry may be, it can still be turned off in the very beginning, and turned off pleasantly and effectively. "I wear a wedding ring at work," Gail said. "I'm not married, but no one except Personnel knows that, and they're discreet. Whenever I feel that old chemical magic, I begin to play with my ring. I drop a few imaginary facts about my imaginary husband if the ring doesn't work, how fond he is of rifle practice—it usually is very effective.

"If for any reason I don't want to turn it off, I tell him the truth in confidence. That's very flattering, because it tells him I trust him."

A rising young executive we knew with an abundance of charm had another method. He was married but didn't wear a wedding ring. "Rings bother me, but if a situation becomes awkward, I very quickly get out pictures of my wife and kids and tell them stories about my kids' orthodontia. It usually works—only usually because there's always one kook who's turned on by a married man who seems unavailable."

The trick in all of this, a psychiatrist told us when we discussed the problem with him, is to know what you want. "If you want an illicit affair, then all the tricks in the world won't work, because your unconscious body language will be shouting, *I do! I do!* You may think you don't want to get involved because reason tells you it's no good or dangerous or inappropriate, but in your heart you may still want it. For heart read unconscious. Dangerous as the flirtation may be, it can still be exciting and stimulating. As one patient of mine put it, it's one time when you really come alive.

"Sexual chemistry, he tells me, is not something you should resist. It's rare and wonderful. Now with an attitude like his you may want to turn it off intellectually, but sure as hell you'll keep it turned on emotionally."

VIRGINS AND DEVILS

"When I want to control sexual chemistry—not necessarily turn it off, but keep it going at the pace I want—I dress accordingly, in significant colors," Melissa, a fashion designer, told us.

We asked her what she meant by significant colors, and she frowned a moment, then nodded. "Okay, let's start with black and white. I know they're not truly colors, but I think of them as colors in terms of clothes. White is virginal, pure, innocent, immaculate. If I want to come on like that I wear a white dress, the longer the better. Of course, some men are turned on by virginal white, but others are turned off. You have to know your man.

"Now if I want to encourage whatever sexual chemistry is going on, I'll try black. A simple black dress, high-necked. That's very sexy, especially if the back is cut low. A low-cut black dress, a cocktail dress, can be sexy too, but it's a broader statement, more obvious, and so is a strapless black dress.

"To be sexy, black must be revealing, or it must hold a promise of revealing, such as a dress cut low with a touch of lace to hide the cleavage."

"Does the black and white apply to men too?" we asked.

"Sure. If white is virginal, then black is rather devilish. A black turtleneck on a man is very sexy. Black leather is sexy with a hint of violence, and of course black evening clothes give the impression of a man of the world."

Looking for a connection between Melissa's ideas of color and sexiness and Dr. Lee's ideas about color and love, we asked, "What about red?"

"Red is daring. The fallen woman would wear red, the experienced woman, the woman who knows her way around. Red is your experienced lover." We nodded. That agreed with Dr. Lee's definition of *eros*.

"And blue?"

"Oh, blue is a cool color, laidback. It signals someone who has it all under control. Blue-eyed people favor blue, of course, and blue-eyed people are easier to read in terms of sexual chemistry. You can tell when they're turned on."

"You'd better explain that."

"It's body language. Large pupils mean someone is interested in you, and with blue eyes you can distinguish the pupils very easily. Small pupils signify coldness, disinterest. You can't read the language of pupils in black-eyed or brown-eyed women. They merge into the iris, but in a blue-eyed woman they're very distinct. That's why blue-eyed blonds are often considered cold."

"And just as often considered sexy."

"Oh well, no one reads people perfectly."

"What about yellow in clothes?"

"Yellow is bright, cheerful, sunny, and light, and a yellow dress or blouse conveys that. You see, you can send almost any signal you want by the color of your clothes."

12
Mirroring and Mentors

THE MIRRORING PROCESS

In the course of trying to uncover some of the reasons why sexual chemistry occurs, we talked with Dr. Massao Miyamoto, assistant professor of psychiatry at Cornell Medical College, New York Hospital. Dr. Miyamoto is a specialist in crosscultural aspects of narcissism and borderline personalities. According to Dr. Miyamoto, sexual chemistry is often based on an initial attraction that is a function of what he describes as a mirroring process.

When we asked him to explain a mirroring process, he said, "It may be the brilliance of the other person's mind, the way he talks, his face or body—or even some sort of sexual energy. This is, in a sense, an idealization of the person, but in the beginning of a relationship it is very powerful and enhancing.

"Of course, as we get to know the person better the idealization wears off. The object of our sexual chemistry, we discover, has feet of clay and becomes, to our disappointment, an ordinary human being.

"Now if we are well adjusted and mature, it's just as easy to love someone with feet of clay. We all have them, and the chemistry with a real person can be just as satisfying as it is with an idealization. In fact, it can be easier to love someone when we find out what they're really like, when we come to know their faults as well as their virtues."

What intrigued us about Dr. Miyamoto's ideas was his concept of a mirroring process, the theory that sexual chemistry acts at its best when you see in someone else a characteristic you either possess or want to possess in yourself. Is this necessarily a function of sexual chemistry between a man and a woman, or can it occur between two men or two women?

One of our premises about sexual chemistry is that it can occur in the same sex, between two men or two women, and with this in mind we began to look for examples of it that incorporated the mirroring process.

In one of our interviews, we talked to Madeline, a young divorced mother with a small child. Her husband had left her before the birth of her daughter, and now she was raising the child alone.

"I manage to cope," she told us. "It's not easy, and if it weren't for Stella I don't know how I'd have done it. Finding a job after being a housewife for five years, taking care of my baby, the problems of day care—it was overwhelming!

"I met Stella while I was still in the hospital. She was a maternity nurse, and something sprang up between us at once, an instant liking. She used to come in while I was nursing the baby and we'd talk endlessly, about everything. When I left the hospital there was no question but that we'd stay friends.

"It seemed to me that Stella had all the strength and

courage that I wanted and needed so desperately—and she was able to give it to me, to strengthen my own resolve to make it, to look for work and become self-supporting. I just couldn't have made it without her."

In Stella Madeline found, if not a mirror image of herself, an image of what she could be, of what she wanted to be. They became very close, very intimate, but in a psychological, not physical, sense. "There'd be long, wonderful evenings of talk in which we'd reveal our deepest feelings to each other," Madeline said. "If there was any emergency, I could always call Stella—and she could call me. She was, in many ways, the kind of friend my husband should have been. Was there sexual chemistry between us? Yes, but there was never anything physical. It was not that kind of a relationship."

THE HELP OF OUR FRIENDS

This deep, helping friendship between two women is seen more often today than ever before, especially as divorce becomes easier and women are less apt to be locked into bad marriages for life. But the newly single woman, often with a child, can find herself adrift in an alien ocean. She has to face a new and frightening independence alone, and she often finds in another woman the friendship, strength, and support to keep going.

Men have less of a need for the help of their friends, especially friends who are men. Independence is an accepted part of life for men in this society, and most of them achieve it readily. While divorce and a return to single life may be shattering, it doesn't bring the same problems that women face. There is the problem of loneliness, but men tend to solve this with work, and there also are more women available to the single man. Women in the same situation are either reluctant to become involved again or find that the available men grow fewer and fewer as they grow older.

But still, same-sex friendships and incidents of intense sexual chemistry between men occur very frequently. In their adolescent years boys develop close, deep friendships with other boys. Men alone in their occupations, deprived of the company of women—cowboys, ranchers, sheepherders, oil-rig workers—drift into friendships that can be almost caricatures of marriage, with all the jealousies, bickerings, and love, but without the sex.

Bret Harte, in his short stories of prospectors in the Old West, particularly in the story "Uncle Jim and Uncle Billy," portrays, beautifully and sensitively, the deep sexual chemistry that can develop between two isolated men. In our own study, Hal, one of the men we interviewed, said he had experienced this same type of friendship at work.

"I was running a medical laboratory, and we hired someone, not a trained technician, but just a man who could help out in general, sort of a chief cook and bottle washer. Johnny got the job. He was a pleasant-enough guy, not too well educated, but a willing worker.

"The first day I worked with him, showing him the procedures, I felt a quick sense of response, a willingness that impressed me—and there was an air about him, a kind of independence I admired. I come from a protective family, and Johnny, to me, seemed to have a wonderful quality of always landing on his feet. He learned the work very quickly, and began instituting his own, rather good systems.

"We began to go out after work for a few beers, and we'd talk—or I'd talk and Johnny would listen—and sometimes we'd drift on to a singles bar and pick up a few girls for the evening. That was something Johnny was very smooth at. There was a quality about him that attracted people, men and women. Part of it was his looks, and part his manner. For an uneducated guy he was very smooth, very self-assured.

"I liked him for that, for qualities I didn't have but very much wanted, and he, as he told me one night when we had had a good many drinks, liked me for my brain. 'You're a guy I can sit and listen to for hours, Hal,' he said. 'I'd give anything to be like you!' "

In Hal's friendship with Johnny, there was a clear case of the mirroring that Dr. Miyamoto spoke to us about. Both men were attracted to qualities in the other that they wanted in themselves. "The trouble was," Hal told us, "we finally became too close—I guess you can say unhealthily close."

"In what way?" we asked.

Frowning, he said, "It got to the point where we were seeing so much of each other, almost every night, that I think both of us were afraid."

"But afraid of what?" we persisted.

Hal shrugged, embarrassed. "I guess, to be blunt, we were afraid of it turning into a homosexual affair. Now don't get me wrong. Neither of us is gay, but it's just that we both, mutually, began to back away from the friendship just because we didn't want it to be physical. We pretty much cooled it, and though we both still work together, and I like Johnny as much as ever, it's just . . . well, one of those things."

A FEAR OF FRIENDSHIP

What Hal had so much difficulty putting into words was spelled out for us by Dr. Althea Horner, a psychoanalyst and an associate clinical professor of psychiatry at Mount Sinai School of Medicine. "Most people," she explained, "are frightened of same-sex friendships. The fear is that eventually they may have to act it out."

"And by acting it out . . ."

"I mean have an actual sexual affair with their friend. Usually, however, men in groups or pairs can discharge this fear of sex in different symbolic ways."

"Such as?"

"Well, the body contact of punching and shoving and, in general, roughhousing. You see a lot of that among men, especially adolescents. You see a lot of it in professional athletics, where men depend on each other for winning fantastic amounts of money. There's the friendly pat on the butt in football after a good play. It's a symbolic way of getting in the physical contact they want, and it's perfectly acceptable in our culture. Among women there's a bit less of a problem in discharging it, because hugging and kissing, even hand-holding in public, are allowed.

"There's also another factor at work here that makes it more difficult for a man to have a close, deep friendship with another man, like your friends Hal and Johnny. This is the whole problem of gender identification. A woman, raised by her mother, has no trouble identifying with other women. She has the example of her mother. A man, raised by his mother, often feels the need to break with the feminine force that raised him in order to assert his masculinity.

"He must also break with the feminine force within himself. Thus, he may see a close male friend as something of a threat. He may come to fear the possibility of sexual chemistry with another man because it would downgrade his manhood. Your friend Hal, from what you told me of his background—studious, bright, not very independent—could well have had such problems, and felt that the only solution to the gathering closeness of his attraction to Johnny was breaking off or cooling the friendship."

"Are there any other ways such close friendships can be handled?" we asked.

Dr. Horner shrugged. "When you have that strong, intense sexual chemistry occurring between two people of the same sex—and believe me, it occurs very often—you have three options—no, four options, for one is to accept it and get the most out of it, be happy in the friendship and learn from it."

That was what Madeline had done in her friendship with her friend Stella. She had continued to remain close, gathering strength and support from her friend. Hal could not do it with Johnny.

"It's always harder for a man because of the gender-identity problem," Dr. Horner assured us. "In our culture men usually have a morbid fear of homosexuality, even if there is no strong element of it in their own makeup."

"What are the other three ways of handling these close attractions?"

"Aside from enjoying them? Well, you can act them out symbolically; with men it's rough-and-tumble sports, physical punching and clowning around, and with women hugging, kissing, and touching. Or you can flee

from them, as Hal did—break off the friendship because
it's becoming too close, too dangerous."

"And the third alternative?"

She smiled. "I suppose you'd call that 'go with the
flow.' Have the sexual affair."

"Do you recommend that?"

"I'm not recommending anything. I'm simply saying
that these are the ways that you can handle sexual
chemistry when it occurs with someone of the same sex,
when it becomes very strong and reaches the stage you
consider dangerous. You can accept it, discharge your
feelings symbolically, flee from it—or act it out."

THE MENTOR RELATIONSHIP

There is a particular kind of sexual chemistry that can
happen between two people of the same sex, or between
people of different sexes. This is the mentor-protégé relationship. We have seen an example of it in the friendship
between Madeline and Stella, an older, mature woman
who lends strength and support to a younger one.

In a Hollywood movie of the forties, *Deception,* the
mentor-protégé theme forms the basis of the plot. Bette
Davis, a music student, believes her husband, Paul
Henreid, is dead, and she is taken under the wing of
Claude Rains, a sophisticated conductor who acts as
mentor to her. Her husband eventually returns, and a
triangle develops because the mentor relationship has
deepened to jealous love.

This, of course, is the basic danger behind any mentor-
protégé situation, whatever the sexes of the people in-

volved. What starts as a teacher helping and guiding a pupil can all too easily change to a lover helping and guiding a loved one, because there is almost always an element of love between mentor and protégé. The danger of love becomes greater as the creative force of the mentor guides the career and creates a new and strong personality in the student.

The classic myth of Pygmalion and Galatea has elements of the mentor-protégé relationship. Pygmalion carves Galatea out of ivory, and is so inspired by his creation that he falls in love with her. The story ends happily with the goddess Aphrodite breathing life into the cool ivory of Galatea, and she steps down from her pedestal into Pygmalion's arms.

The growth of love in this relationship is not always a danger. Sometimes it is solved very simply. We know an English teacher, a widower in his sixties, who had a very promising woman student. He encouraged her and helped her, advised her and took a deep interest in her work. Eventually she began to publish, and eventually she also fell in love with him. There was a thirty-year difference in their ages, but she insisted that it made no difference. Against his better judgment and the advice of their friends they did marry, and the marriage has so far been a happy and satisfying one.

"As long as she can be a protégé," Dr. Horner said, commenting on this story, "I think the marriage can work. She doesn't have to challenge him. He can continue in the mentor relationship. But if she in effect grows up and matures I can see trouble ahead. Often the mentor cannot tolerate his protégé's growing up and becoming independent."

With George and Tony the relationship went differently. George was a bartender at a very popular bar in town, and Tony was a busboy in the restaurant that adjoined it. Young, eager, and brash, Tony struck a responsive chord in George, and a quick sexual chemistry sprang up between them. George had been working at this bar for ten years and was not only an excellent bartender but a superb fount of advice and comfort to the regulars. It was this quality in him that appealed to Tony.

One day Tony approached him and asked if he'd teach him how to tend bar. "There's no future in bussing," Tony said glimly, "and I'll never get to be a waiter in this place."

George was older, divorced, and somewhat lonely. Tony was like the son he had never had, and George became a good father to him. Gradually the chemistry between them deepened. George taught Tony his skills, and persuaded the management to give him a chance at the bar. "I really need some help," he insisted, and it was true. With George's help and advice Tony got better and better at the job. He picked up George's knack of listening, and was particularly good with the single women.

"I'm really proud of the kid," George confided to his friends, and he was. After all, Tony was his creation, as far as bartending went.

It all hit the fan, however, when Tony announced to George that he was moving on to a much better paying job at a new restaurant opening across town. "There's a real future in it for me."

George nodded, but from then on until Tony left he was curt and cold. Tony, bewildered, couldn't understand what was happening. He had been so sure George would be pleased by his opportunity, and instead he discovered that he had lost a friend—one of the best friends he had ever made.

"It was a clear case," Dr. Horner explained when we

told her about them, "of the protégé growing up and becoming independent. That's something the mentor, no matter how strong the sexual chemistry between them is, cannot tolerate."

In a really good mentor relationship, when the sexual chemistry carries them along, things are terrific. What it becomes is an idealization of the parent-child situation, but eventually the child, as any child does, must learn to stand on his own feet. The independence of the protégé can be as traumatic to the mentor as the independence of the child is to the parent.

Many parents cannot accept this, and the only way the child reaches independence is by making an angry break with them. In the same way, the protégé must often make an angry break with his mentor in order to stand on his own feet. Tony went on to a successful career in another restaurant, and eventually was able to raise enough money to start his own place. Instead of being able to take pride in what his protégé had done, George refused to discuss or hear about Tony's good luck. He simply cut him out of his life.

POLITICAL SEDUCTION

The sexual chemistry that results in the mentor-protégé relationship is similar in many ways to the chemistry that can occur between a politician and his constituents. There are some of the same elements present: a strong, charismatic figure who offers us guidance and hope, someone we can rely on and trust.

It seems that there is something built into our personalities that impels us to react with hero worship and trust or love to any strong, charm-filled individual who offers us pie right here on earth instead of in the sky by-and-by. Perhaps the key lies in our childhood, when we became accustomed to an authority figure in the home who was the source of all our benefits and held the answer to all our wishes. In a way, when we react to the sexual chemistry of a politician, we are only reacting to a carry-over of the authority figure of Mom or Dad.

Humans seem to need a leader, and once committed to one by whatever sexual chemistry he uses, they are will-ing to follow him all the way. We even accept the fact that a political leader can tell us to give up our lives for our country, just as we accept whatever economic entangle-ments he gets us into. The acceptance isn't always whole-hearted, and in many cases we fight it. For most of us, the sexual chemistry won't survive a Watergate, but for some it will and does.

The sexual chemistry that a politician uses in seducing an audience involves a great deal of what Dr. Miyamoto called mirror imaging. The politician shows himself in a way that the audience would like to be. This is one reason why image is such a desperately important part of politi-cal manipulation and why men who promise to spruce up the image of a candidate are in such high demand.

Sometimes they are lucky, as when the image has been packaged and sold beforehand, when a national hero or an actor becomes a politician. At other times the image maker will produce a book to detail the courageous past of a candidate, or his philosophical strengths.

The making of these myths is particularly important, but the politician must rely on other details to get his seduction of the public going. His body language must be convincing and smooth, his voice able to charm and convince the audience. President Johnson, when he came to power at the death of the particularly charismatic Kennedy, had graceless, awkward body language. His early TV appearances were wooden and stiff, but gradually, under the tutelage of an image maker, he improved, and by the time he left office he was convincing and smooth and capable of igniting sexual chemistry. President Nixon achieved reasonably smooth body language, but no amount of training could soften his features. His seduction of the voters had to rely on a raw kind of power he exuded.

This worked because power can create a particularly strong sexual chemistry between a politician and the voter. People in general love power of any sort. Any mini-series on TV that features a powerful and ruthless protagonist has a good chance of success.

Power can be seductive. Many of us, once we taste it, can get high on it. It works, in sexual chemistry, through a process of identification. When you have a strong man addressing the nation—a Hitler, a Mussolini, a Franco, a Stalin, an F.D.R., a Churchill—people seduced by his power attach themselves to him. In a way, they become an extension of him and his power. It also helps the sexual chemistry to give the audience the accoutrements of power, the uniforms and parades, the flags and slogans.

To the men in power the adulation of the masses can give a genuine high, but it can be a very lonely high. The sexual chemistry works at a distance. There may be a fleeting touch now and then, but no more than that. They become isolated individuals, and they must, unless

they are capable of enormous self-deceit, understand that
the virtues attributed to them do not really exist. Their
followers are reacting to the power they wield, not to
them.

THE WORLD'S A STAGE

The way in which an actor relates to his audience, a
Broadway actor told us, is very much the way a politician
relates to the voters. "It's a matter of seduction, particularly if you're playing the role of a lover onstage. You are
holding up a distorting mirror to the audience, at least to
those who are the same sex that you are. It's distorted
because it does not mirror reality, but mirrors what
they'd wish to be themselves. That plus a little bit of
themselves as they really are. Without those two elements
on the stage, there can be no sexual chemistry. There
must be enough reality in your acting to create a sense of
identity, and enough fantasy to create a sense of 'that's
what I'd like to be.'

"Of course, sexual chemistry with the audience of the
other sex is somewhat different. You must be recogniz-
able in terms of reality, you must have some element of
someone they love, admire, or know, but there must also
be that identification, the wish to have you make love to
them. In a sense, you *are* making love to them. It's a
process of seduction using sexual chemistry."

"But how do you use it specifically?" we asked.

"There are a number of ways, and oddly enough, your
face is the least of them. I've known some powerfully ugly
men who can turn on an audience sexually in a matter of

minutes. Primarily it's your voice, the message you send over and above the words and the meaning of those words."

"Metacommunication?"

"Whatever. I know an actor who has a cute little schtick. He recites a string of vegetable names in French, and any woman listening to him, if she doesn't understand French, will respond sexually. He puts a caress into every word, an implication, a promise. He's talking gobbledygook, but he turns a woman on. If he can do that with vegetables, imagine what he does with a real part!"

"And beyond the voice?"

"Well, the second most important element is your body language onstage, the way you position yourself, your gesture, your expression, your eye contact. No one has ever created sexual chemistry without eye contact— and onstage you're faced with a blank, dark theater full of people.

"Yet the clever actor gives every person in the audience the illusion that he's making eye contact with him or her alone. It's difficult because that vast, dark mass out there can scare the pants off you at first. But get a reaction, a stir, a ripple of laughter, a sigh, a burst of applause, and suddenly they're with you. The spurt of sexual chemistry has been struck and you're with them.

"And then of course there's movement. I separate that from body language because it's so vital an element. I think it's vital not only on the stage but in every situation where you expect to start some chemistry with another person or a group of people, no matter what the sex."

"Can you tell us what you mean by movement?"

He spread his arms helplessly. "How do you describe it? Part of it is your lightness on your feet, the way you carry yourself, the grace of each movement, how it slides into the next. I can portray a man of eighty just by my walk, or a kid of twenty-one by the way I get out of a chair. I've seen aging actresses play Juliet convincingly by moving as a teenager moves.

"I'll tell you a trade secret that was told to me by Albert Basserman, the world-famous Viennese actor. He said, 'The most important thing about acting is that you stand on the stage with the weight of your body in your legs, not in your head. Your weight must be toward the center of the earth, when you stand, when you move. Remember that!' I've never forgotten it, though I was only a kid at the time. It's the secret of movement that all the greats use—Brando, Tracy, all of them.

"You know," he finished thoughtfully, "I'd advise any aspiring actor to learn dance first, but I'd give the same advice to politicians!"

A friend of ours with a considerable reputation as a lover read through our interview with the actor and said, "What he talked about, movement—he's right, you know. It's the real key to sexual chemistry. Never mind using it onstage. Use it on a one-to-one level, and the way you move is going to transmit a pretty heavy message about yourself.

"That business of standing with the weight of your body in your legs. That signals assurance, competence— but you have to do it with grace. Dance is the key, dance and movement."

13
Effects and Stages

SYNCHRONY: THE GOOD MATCH

"What I can't stand," Ellen said, "is a man with a line. That character over there just finished telling me what beautiful bones I had in my face and did I ever think of being a model. Now I ask you!"

Joan looked at her critically. "Well, you have good bones, and you might make a model at that—if you dropped twenty pounds. But honestly, Ellen, you're too hard on guys. What's wrong with a line?"

"What's wrong?" Ellen stared at her. "Why, it's dishonest and phony, and anyway, it's just a way of breaking the ice."

"Exactly," Joan said triumphantly. "Breaking the ice. That's all it is. I know that most of the guys are just as shy as we are, just as worried about what we'll say to them, and they all think a line will help—and it does. I can't begin to know a guy, let alone like him, until he makes some effort to communicate. That's what a line is, an effort to communicate."

Joan was right. The "line" so many women abhor is the first step in a process that can eventually lead to sexual chemistry. The second step is the searching that goes on after the line breaks the ice. The searching is an attempt to reach a common ground, to discover similar likes and dislikes. It begins an interpersonal relationship that eventually can lead to synchrony.

There can hardly be any sexual chemistry without some synchrony between the two partners. The synchrony can start at the first meeting, the bar where Ellen finally gave in and talked to the good-looking guy with the line. Later it became "their" bar, and the teasing about her being model material was taken up again and became "their" joke. The jukebox song that they played five times that night became "their" song. A synchrony was established as the sexual chemistry grew.

In later meetings, there was an exclusivity. They became an item among their friends. They moved in together and talked marriage. It was a time of closeness, when the sexual chemistry between them was at its peak. They became exclusive to each other, went everywhere as a couple, and began to structure their lives in terms of each other.

Unfortunately, there are times when this closeness can be destructive. Each one of the couple begins to lose a sense of identity as they are swallowed up in the relationship. The boundaries to their egos fade away, and each takes on the opinions of the other. Usually the weaker of the two—in our culture that's often the woman—takes on the likes and dislikes of the stronger. She gives in to her lover and submerges her opinions in his.

Sexual chemistry, once a bond, now becomes a handicap. "I need more space" is the common complaint, and then there is an effort to establish each one's uniqueness.

Occasionally it can be done within the framework of the relationship, but all too often it means breaking up the union to give each a chance to "be himself."

If this distancing and rediscovery of the self can be done in the framework of a marriage or a committed relationship, it will deepen and strengthen it. Sexual chemistry will not only endure, it will become stronger and subtler, developing nuances that hardly existed before.

But if the distancing cannot be done within the structure of the relationship, then splitting up or divorce may be the only answer. This can be done very consciously. Ellen calls her friend and says, "Look, we have to stop seeing each other for a while. I've got to find myself, discover where I'm at. I still love you, but . . ."

Or it can be done unconsciously, by picking fights and arguments to erode the fabric of the intimacy, or by entering into an affair with someone else and letting your partner find out about it. Which is the more effective depends on the personalities of the people involved and also on whether you wish to renew the affair at some later date.

THE EAGER AND RELUCTANT LOVERS

There are times when the "need for space" doesn't arise and when the initial sexual chemistry can be made to last, if not for a lifetime, then for much longer than usual. One method is the "eager lover" or "Romeo and Juliet effect." The two of us against the world! If parental opposition to the affair is strong, or if social pressure is heavy, the couple may decide to give each other up, but more often this kind of pressure from society, from their parents or peers, simply strengthens the bonds created by sexual chemistry and, by isolating the lovers from the world, drives them closer together. The little things that might have broken up the affair early on, that might have sent them looking for a chance to be themselves, are seen as much less important than the attempts of the outside world to destroy their love, and so these things are over-looked. What could have ended an affair if everyone left them alone just brings them closer together as everyone tries to separate them.

Another thing that can sometimes strengthen or even ignite sexual chemistry is the "reluctant lover effect." Is a reluctant lover more desirable than an eager one? Will sexual chemistry, if it occurs with a reluctant lover, be stronger and more intense than if it occurs with someone who is an easy conquest? According to Cathy, it will.

Cathy, in her early twenties, is a very beautiful woman. "I've never had any trouble getting acquainted with a man," she told us. "I'd make eye contact and smile, and the rest came naturally. I know it's the way I look. It sort of bowls men over, but I don't take any credit for that. My looks are no part of my own doing. I was born this way—but I do use my looks, and they pay off.

"The thing is, I never worry about sexual chemistry. It happens often enough, and when it's over, it's over. Easy come, easy go. And then I met Adam. I want to tell you, he was something else, bright and talented. He's a nature photographer, and a good one. He sells to all the maga-zines." She hesitated, then smiled ruefully. "To tell you the truth, the thing about him that attracted me is that he seemed so totally unimpressed with my looks. He's just about the first man I met who didn't seem to give a damn what I looked like. I couldn't get over it. I just didn't turn him on! There was no sexual chemistry.

"That got to me, and I realized I was taking all men for granted. I set out very deliberately to turn Adam on. I was charming and sexy and I used every trick I knew, and eventually it worked, but I really had to put myself out, and you know, now Adam means more to me than any man I've gone with. I'm very serious about him, very."

What Cathy found out in her efforts to attract Adam is a fact that's been known to researchers in psychology for a long time: the reluctant lover is the most desirable. The reasoning goes, if I must put myself out to get him, he must really be worth something.

It's a bit like the song from *Patience* about the magnet who hung in a hardware shop. Scissors and needles and knives were all attracted to him, but he set his heart on a silver churn because she would have none of him. The magnet reasoned, "If I can wheedle a knife or needle, then why not a silver churn?" The reluctant lover was the most desirable.

Then should you play hard to get if you want to heat up your quotient of sexual chemistry? In a sense, yes—but with many qualifications. Just how hard to get you should play is one qualification. The very phrase *hard to get* is another. *Selective* is a much better concept. The person who is selective is usually more desirable. Someone who gives in at once is usually too easy a victory.

Dr. Elaine Walster and her associates reported in the *Journal of Personality and Social Psychiatry* the results of a study in which they attempted to sort out the pros and cons of playing hard to get. They described an experiment in which men telephoned three women with whom they were supposedly computer-matched. One woman appeared eager to date anyone; another was just the opposite, not eager to date any of the men. The third was eager to date one man, but not the rest. The selective woman, the one eager to date only one specific man, was the most popular of the group.

The researchers concluded that a woman or man who is "selectively reticent" when first approached is most attractive. The moral: sexual chemistry works best when you appear reluctant with everyone but the man or woman of your choice.

MISREADING THE SIGNALS

"When I want to create some sexual chemistry," Meg told us, "I use the ricochet effect." When we pressed her to explain, she said, "When I'm in a singles bar, or at a party or social get-together, I try to avoid just sitting and waiting for someone to talk to me. No one wants to approach a person who just sits there glumly, or your basic 'cool' type who looks as if she doesn't give a damn whether anyone talks to her or not. It's a defense, of course, but it comes across as self-involvement, and it usually turns everyone off.

"I know that when I see a man ignoring everyone around him I mentally shrug and ignore him too. I figure that's what he wants. Sure, he may just be shy or frightened or insecure, but who has time to analyze all that? Who wants to take a chance and be stuck with a dud? So I look around for someone who seems to be having fun.

"Now that's where the ricochet effect comes in. When

I go barhopping, I try to be approachable. I talk to people, to the bartender, to the person next to me. At a party I join a group and speak up, act friendly and smile. In other words, I'm approachable. It always works. I give off the right vibes, the impression that here's someone you can talk to easily, someone who won't freeze you out or turn you off.

"In a way, you're putting yourself on exhibit, letting your personality ricochet off someone else, saying, in effect, 'Look, I'm available, amusing, easy to talk to, and easy to get along with. Try me'—and it's amazing how many people do!"

Meg is right. Men and women are judged by how they appear, by the personality they show to others. The image they project will ricochet off the one they are talking to, to anyone else in the room looking for a partner or for someone to spend some time with.

But judging a person solely by appearance can often be misleading. Are you judging what that person really is or the image he or she projects? It takes some acuity to separate the image from reality. To a young woman watching the Calvin Klein advertisements for jeans, no bra and a tight pair of jeans can simply mean she is in style. To a young man, the same commercial can mean the woman dressed like that is ready for sex. There is a sexual difference in perception.

"My first date with Paul," Gail complained, "was a disaster. I liked him a lot, but my God, he came on like Godzilla—and I don't know why. I certainly didn't encourage him."

"Encourage me?" Paul shook his head. "That kid shouldn't be allowed out of the house alone. I picked her up to go dancing at a disco down on Santa Monica and she's wearing short shorts and a tank top without a bra. What was I supposed to think? And then we got to talking in the car and I couldn't shut up. I felt that if I didn't talk I'd make a grab at her! So I began talking to her about astronomy—that's my hobby—and pointing out the constellations, and she said maybe we could park and I could show her some. I ask you, what was I supposed to do?''

"I didn't lead him on," Gail protested. "I was genuinely interested in what he was saying, like I really dig astrology, and I never knew which was which. He was so smart and I was fascinated. All I wanted was for him to point out the Gemini—that's my sign.''

And so it went, a complete misunderstanding of sexual signals. Both Gail and Paul were teenagers, and the misunderstanding is not surprising. According to a study by four Los Angeles researchers at UCLA, boys still read more sexual come-ons into girls' behavior than the girls intend. The researchers, four women, quizzed over four hundred teenagers about the signals of sexual chemistry that young men and women send out. The interesting fact that emerged was that men were likely to see a sexual come-on in almost every situation.

Young women failed to see sexual come-ons in either clothes or where a date took place. None of them thought open shirts, tight pants, or jewelry on a man was an invitation to sex.

But men felt that with women, a see-through blouse, low-cut tops, tight jeans, no bra were all invitations to sex. Men also seemed to see the same invitation in every situation, whether it was a date in a public place or an evening at home alone. They also felt that talking about sex, saying "I love you" or telling the man how good-looking he was, and even looking into his eyes were all sexual come-ons!

This more hyped-up, teenage, male view of sexuality persists, to an extent, beyond the teens. In general, men are more prone to interpret innocent signals as sexual invitations. The reason? Some researchers feel it may be glandular. Teenage boys are more tuned into sex than girls. Kinsey showed that men are in their sexual prime in their late teens; women reach it much later.

But the UCLA research team thinks it's a function of the fact that women have more to lose from sexual activity—pregnancy or a bad reputation. Whatever the reason, women entering the dating scene should be aware that innocent reactions and clothes they think are simply stylish may be adding fuel to latent sexual chemistry. They can use this knowledge to tone down the chemistry—or, if they wish, to keep it going.

Gail and Paul were teenagers, and it can be argued that in the teens we easily send out the wrong signals or fail to interpret the right signals. Teenagers still have a lot to learn. But sexual chemistry can be just as confusing to an older man or woman, especially when one fails to understand the signals one is sending to others.

Florence, a teacher, was in her early thirties, a good-looking woman, but far from an overwhelming beauty. Yet her constant complaint was that men always thought she was coming on to them. "I really don't," she told us earnestly. "It just seems that every man I meet makes a pass at me, even when I don't want it. I don't think I'm doing anything to encourage them."

We agreed to watch Florence during a lunch date she had with a male teacher at her school. They sat in the cafeteria, and we were able to get a table a short distance away from which we could see her clearly and overhear her without being seen ourselves. Watching and listening for half an hour convinced us that indeed Florence was doing something she was unaware of, was in fact flirting very openly with her fellow teacher, although nothing in what she said gave any indication of a sexual come-on. By the time lunch was over there was a very strong sexual chemistry going between them, but we could see that she was completely bewildered when the man suggested that they go out that evening.

What had Florence done? By her body language and her metacommunication she had sent out a constant series of signals: *I am available.* To begin with, she smiled throughout the lunch, and though she faced her fellow teacher, she would frequently look down, averting her eyes—a sign of submission in body language. The sexual dance between men and women is often predicated on a symbolic act of submission by the woman and dominance by the man.

Florence would lean forward from time to time and tilt her head to one side as she listened to her friend, and every once in a while she would flex her shoulders. What she said to him was matter-of-fact, but she said it in a high-pitched but soft voice.

If she disagreed with anything her friend said, she at once sent a signal of submission, looking down and raising her shoulders. She used preening gestures frequently: pushing her hair back into place, cocking her head to one side, stretching.

All in all, she behaved seductively. As we listened it became clear that this behavior was defensive, an attempt to cut off any possible hostility on the part of her fellow teacher.

We didn't know where Florence's defensive behavior originated. Possibly it was in her childhood, as a defense against a too-strict father. At any rate, her problems with men were beyond our ability to handle. All we could do was point out some of her basic mistakes that led to the flirtatious, seductive way she handled herself with men. Once she learned to stop, she would have some control over the sexual chemistry she was so adept at creating.

THE COURTSHIP DANCE

No book on sexual chemistry would be complete without some explanation of the routine, or dance, that we all go through when we want to set sexual chemistry in motion, when we want to ignite that special spark with someone we find attractive. We have given the elements that go into sexual chemistry, the image projection, techniques to turn it on and off, the reasons for it and methods of handling it, but it would help all of us, as it helped Florence, to understand the exact body language that goes on between a man and a woman who find each other attractive.

In a very comprehensive article in *Psychiatry* on the nonverbal basis of attraction, Dr. David B. Givens of the University of Washington has outlined the body language of flirtation. He lists five courtship stages that lead to sexual chemistry. As an example, he cites a man who sits down at a table in a cafeteria across from an attractive woman.

The Attention Stage

First there is a civil nod, by which the man and woman acknowledge each other's presence. The woman is reading a book and, outside of the nod of recognition, doesn't glance at the man, but he is attracted to her. Hesitant to approach her, as most men would be, he begins a series of unconscious body-language maneuvers. He faces his body toward her, but doesn't look at her directly. Instead, he looks around, often crossing her field of vision. She, aware of him now, may meet his eyes briefly. It is likely he would smile and tilt his head back and shake it from side to side, a "head toss." He might then touch himself—his arm, his face, his chest.

A slight anxiety may cause him to yawn, stretch, extend his arms toward the woman, flex or raise his arms, swell out his chest, scratch his face, adjust his tie, finger his hair. He may lower his gaze, smile, look at the woman, and then look away.

The Recognition Stage

The woman now may take one of two courses. She can discourage him by turning away, refusing to meet his eyes, or staring at him blankly. If she wishes to encourage him, she may turn toward him, make eye contact, raise her eyebrows, touch her face, and lower her eyes demurely. She might toss her head and like him stretch, yawn, swell her chest, push her hair back, smile, or even bat her eyelashes, blink rapidly. She may also begin to touch herself—her arms and body.

The Interaction Stage

If all goes well as far as this, the next step is conversation. Anything can be an opener. "Please pass the salt." "It's a wonderful day out, isn't it?" "That waiter is something else!" "I see you're reading Kierkegaard."

There's a lot of eye contact in this stage. The anxiety increases too. What if he or she says, "Get lost!" There's a bigger chance for humiliation, and so the anxiety signals increase: preening, tossing the head, clearing the throat, stretching, yawning. There might be an overresponse, too much head shaking and nodding, too loud laughing, but as they become aware of each other's interest, synchrony sets in. Each begins to imitate the other's movements.

Their voices tend to become softer and higher in pitch as this phase continues, and eye contact is extended, but also broken frequently by looking down. There is more shrugging, tilting of the head, shoulder flexing, and the palm of the hand is shown more frequently.

The Sexual-Chemistry Stage

If all goes well and sexual chemistry has been ignited, it may lead to the couple's making a date. They will begin to see each other regularly and a more private courtship begins. There is touching, staring, caressing, hand-holding; sometimes a kind of baby talk starts, pet names, cute phrases; and there is a lot of eye-to-eye gazing.

The Resolution Stage

Sexual chemistry is at its height now. Courtship leads to marriage or the bedroom or both, but after sex a distancing usually takes place. The couple behaves as an established pair, and the body language and the courtship signs drop away.

UNDERSTANDING LOVE

We've seen what sexual chemistry is and considered the elements that make it up. Understanding these can help us when the opportunity for sexual chemistry presents itself, or when we want to create that opportunity. Sexual chemistry is not something that happens out of the blue. It's true that often, "across a crowded room," we see that someone special and we feel that we are falling in love. But a lot must go on before that love is reciprocated, and we can make our feelings clear. Knowing the stages of courtship helps, and knowing the elements that make up sexual chemistry helps too. Knowing our inner selves, our fears and desires, helps most of all. Too many of us fear love and turn off sexual chemistry before it begins. We have to learn how to keep it alive and conquer our fears and self-doubts. The old saw is true; it's better to have loved and lost than never to have loved at all. It's better to experience sexual chemistry even if it ends in disaster than to cut it off before it starts, or abort it in the process.

We went through a period of sexual freedom in the seventies, and now, in the eighties, it seems likely from all the signs that sexuality is closing down and morals are tightening up. A general conservative approach is evident not only in politics but in sexuality as well. The free-and-easy sex of a generation ago seems to be dying away, and in today's world we are going to need all the knowledge of how and why and when sexual chemistry works. More than ever, the signals and techniques, the innate chemistry of love, are becoming necessary knowledge.

References

ANDERSEN, CHRISTOPHER. *The Name Game.* New York: Simon & Schuster, 1977.

ARONSON, E., AND LINDEN, D. "Gain and Loss of Esteem as Determinants of Interpersonal Attractiveness." *Journal of Experimental Social Psychology* 1 (1965):156–71.

BACH, GEORGE R., AND DEUTSCH, RONALD M. *Pairing.* New York: Avon Books, 1971.

BENOIT, HUBERT. *The Many Faces of Love.* London: Pantheon Books, 1955.

BIRCH, M. C. *Pheromones.* Amsterdam: North Holland Publishers, 1974.

CALHOUN, JAMES F., AND ACOCELLA, JOAN ROSS. *Psychology of Adjustment and Human Relationships.* New York: Random House, 1983.

CLORE, G. L., WIGGINS, N. H., AND ITKIN, S. "Judging Attraction from Nonverbal Behavior: The Gain Phenomenon." *Journal of Consulting and Clinical Psychology* 43 (1975):491–97.

COMFORT, ALEX. "Likelihood of Human Pheromones." *Nature* 230 (1971):432–79.

CROOKS, ROBERT, AND BAUR, KARLA. *Our Sexuality.* Menlo Park, Calif.: Benjamin-Cummings Publishing Co., 1980.

DION, K. K., AND DION, K. L. "Self-Esteem and Romantic Love." *Journal of Personality* 43 (1975):39–57.

DRISCOLL, R., DAVIS, K. E., AND LIPETZ, M. E. "Parental Interference and Romantic Love: The Romeo and Juliet Effect." *Journal of Personality and Social Psychology* 24 (1972):1–10.

DUTTON, D. G., AND ARON, A. P. "Some Evidence for Heightened Sexual Attraction Under Conditions of High Anxiety." *Journal of Personality and Social Psychology* 30 (1974):510–17.

EIBL-EIBESFELDT, IRENÄUS. *Love and Hate.* New York: Holt, Rinehart & Winston, 1971.

ELLIS, ALBERT. "Rational Psychotherapy." *Journal of General Psychology* 59 (1958):35–49.

ELLIS, HAVELOCK. *Studies in the Psychology of Sex.* New York: Random House, 1936.

FAST, BARBARA. *Getting Close.* New York: G. P. Putnam's Sons, 1978.

FAST, JULIUS. *Body Language.* New York: M. Evans and Co., 1970.

FAST, JULIUS, AND FAST, BARBARA. *Talking Between the Lines.* New York: Viking Press, 1979.

FROMM, ERICH. *The Art of Loving.* New York: Harper & Row, Publishers, 1956.

GIVENS, DAVID B. "The Nonverbal Basis of Attraction: Flirtation, Courtship, and Seduction." *Psychiatry* 41 (1978):346–58.

HAGEN, RICHARD. *The Bio-Sexual Factor.* New York: Doubleday Publishing Co., 1979.

HATFIELD, E., AND WALSTERN, G. W. *A New Look at Love.* Reading, Mass.: Addison-Wesley Publishing Co., 1978.

HESS, E. H. "Attitude and Pupil Size." *Scientific American* 212 (1965):46–54.

HOPSON, JANET. *Scent Signals.* New York: William Morrow & Co., 1979.

JOHNSON, S. M., AND WHITE, G. "Self-Observation as an Agent of Behavioral Change." *Behavior Therapy* 2 (1971): 488–97.

KIRKENDALL, LESTER A., AND WHITEHURST, ROBERT N. *The New Sexual Revolution.* New York: Donald and Brown, 1971.

KIRKPATRICK, C., AND COTTON, J. "Physical Attractiveness, Age and Marital Adjustment." *American Sociological Review* 16 (1951):285–90.

LEE, JOHN ALAN. *Colours of Love.* Toronto: New Press, 1973.

LIEBOWITZ, MICHAEL R. *The Chemistry of Love.* Boston: Little, Brown & Co., 1983.

MASLOW, ABRAHAM. *Toward a Psychology of Being.* Princeton, N.J.: Van Nostrand Reinhold, 1962.

MASTERS, WILLIAM H., AND JOHNSON, VIRGINIA E. *Human Sexual Inadequacy.* Boston: Little, Brown & Co., 1970.

MAY, ROLLO. *Love and Will.* New York: W. W. Norton & Co., 1969.

MEICHENBAUM, DONALD H. *Cognitive Behavior Modification: An Integrative Approach.* New York: Plenum Press, 1977.

MISCHEL, W. "Toward a Cognitive Learning Reconceptualization of Personality." *Psychological Review* 80 (1973): 253–83.

MONEY, JOHN, AND TUCKER, PATRICIA. *Sexual Signatures.* Boston: Little, Brown & Co., 1975.

MORRIS, DESMOND. *Intimate Behavior.* London: Jonathan Cape, 1971.

MURSTEIN, BERNARD. *Love, Sex and Marriage Throughout the Ages.* New York: Springer Publishing Co., 1974.

———. "Self-Ideal Self Discrepancy and the Choice of a Marital Partner." *Journal of Consulting and Clinical Psychology* 37 (1971):47–52.

OFFIT, AVODAH K. *The Sexual Self.* Philadelphia: J. B. Lippincott Co., 1977.

PHILLIPS, DEBORA, AND JUDD, ROBERT. *How to Fall Out of Love.* Boston: Houghton Mifflin Co., 1978.

RESTAK, RICHARD M. *The Brain: The Last Frontier.* New York: Warner Books, 1973.

RUBIN, ZICK. "Loving and Leaving." Paper presented at the Annual Convention of the American Psychological Association, 3–7 September 1976, Washington, D.C.

——. "Measurement of Romantic Love." *Journal of Personality and Social Psychology* 16 (1970):265–73.

SAFILIOS-ROTHSCHILD, CONSTANTINA. *Love, Sex and Sex Roles.* Englewood Cliffs, N.J.: Prentice-Hall, 1977.

SCHACHTER, STANLEY. *The Psychology of Affiliation.* Stanford, Calif.: Stanford University Press, 1969.

SIGALL, H., AND OSTROVE, N. "Beautiful but Dangerous: Effects of Offender Attractiveness and Nature of the Crime on Juridic Judgment." *Journal of Personality and Social Psychology* 31 (1975):410–14.

SOKOLOV, H., HARRIS, R., AND HECKER, M. "Isolation of Substances from Human Vaginal Secretions Previously Shown to Be Sex Attractant Pheromones in Higher Primates." *Archives of Sexual Behavior* 5 (1976):269–74.

TENNOV, DOROTHY. *Love and Limerance.* New York: Stein & Day, Publishers, 1980.

WALSTER, E., WALSTER, G. W., PILIAVIN, J., AND SCHMIDT, L. "Playing Hard to Get: Understanding an Elusive Phenomenon." *Journal of Personality and Social Psychology* 26 (1973):113–21.

WATSON, JOHN B. *Behaviorism.* Chicago: University of Chicago Press, 1924.